Annie Oakley

Annie
Oakley

Chuck Wills

DK PUBLISHING

LONDON, NEW YORK, MUNICH,
MELBOURNE, AND DELHI

Editor : John Searcy
Publishing Director : Beth Sutinis
Designer : Mark Johnson Davies
Art Director : Dirk Kaufman
Photo Research : Anne Burns Images
Production : Ivor Parker
DTP Designer : Kathy Farias

First American Edition, 2007

07 08 09 10 11 10 9 8 7 6 5 4 3 2 1
Published in the United States
by DK Publishing
375 Hudson Street
New York, New York 10014

DK books are available at special discounts
when purchased in bulk for sales
promotions, premiums, fund-raising,
or educational use. For details, contact:

DK Publishing Special Markets
375 Hudson Street
New York, New York 10014
SpecialSales@dk.com

A catalog record for this book is available
from the Library of Congress.

ISBN 978-0-7566-2997-7 (Paperback)
ISBN 978-0-7566-2986-1 (Hardcover)

Printed and bound in Mexico
by R.R. Donnelley

Photography credits:
Front Cover by Getty Images
Back Cover by
Getty Images/Time and Life Pictures

Discover more at
www.dk.com

Contents

"And See Miss Annie Oakley Shooting!"

If you grew up in America in the last decades of the 19th century, or in the first decade of the 20th, the arrival of Buffalo Bill's Wild West in your hometown every year or so was a huge event.

Led by the famous frontiersman William F. Cody, better known as "Buffalo Bill," the show gave audiences a three-hour visit to a time and a place that was already passing into legend—the American West in the era before farms, towns, and railroads filled up the vast lands between the Mississippi River and the West Coast.

Before the day's performance, which usually took place in the afternoon or evening, the whole troupe would parade down the town's main street, with Cody leading the procession. Among them was a woman with a slight physique, clad in a fringed brown dress, leggings, and a broad-brimmed hat. She barely stood out among the cowboys, Indians, and other exotic performers, but—next to Buffalo Bill himself—she was the show's biggest star: Annie Oakley, the most famous female target shooter in the world.

When showtime came, the spectators eagerly took their seats in the local stadium, or in an outdoor arena. The performance usually began with a horse race between the cowboys of various countries. Next, Cody, who was a crack marksman, might do some shooting, blasting hard clay balls with a rifle from horseback.

Then it was Annie's turn.

The excited audience quieted down when Annie entered the arena. At the time, many Americans were familiar with guns. Hunting for food or sport was popular, and in remote places where police forces didn't exist, homeowners often kept a weapon at hand for self defense. Competitive shooting was also a fashionable pastime of the day.

But shooting was supposed to be for men only. Now this small woman was walking to a table where several loaded shotguns were laid out. The heavy weapons looked almost as big as she was. What was she going to do?

When Annie hefted a gun to her

This publicity photo shows Annie with the tools of her trade—from left to right, a pistol, a rifle, and a shotgun.

shoulder and began to shoot, she never failed to dazzle the audience. Despite her size, she handled her gun so easily that it seemed like part of her body—and her aim was astounding. She shattered clay balls thrown in the air or twirled at the end of a cord. Switching to a rifle or pistol, she would snuff out a candle with a bullet or blast the cork out of a bottle—sometimes shooting with the gun over her shoulder, using a mirror to aim. And she didn't just shoot standing up—she also wowed crowds by shooting while riding a bicycle.

Annie never left the arena without the cheers of the crowd ringing in her ears.

The show would go on for about two more hours, with acts like trick roping, simulated buffalo hunts, and staged battles between cowboys and Indians. But as the sun set and the audience filed out of the arena, Annie Oakley's spectacular shooting was what many would remember best.

The popularity of Buffalo Bill's Wild West made Cody one of

Buffalo Bill holds the reins of the Deadwood stagecoach, the centerpiece of one of his most popular acts.

the most famous Americans—perhaps turn of the 20th century. And Annie became one of the most famous American women.

Annie was a fine all-around athlete— as shown in this poster for the Wild West show.

In an era when opportunities for women were limited—when they couldn't even vote in most of the country—her amazing ability with a gun proved that a woman could do just as well (or better) than a man, even in a traditionally "masculine" field like shooting. Annie was indeed glad to be a role model for women—even though she held views about women's place in society that would be considered old-fashioned today.

Of course, there's Annie Oakley the legend, and then there's Annie Oakley the person. It's hard to separate the two. Hundreds of thousands of words were written about Annie in her lifetime and after her death in 1926, but much of what's been written about her is inaccurate or untrue. Only in recent years have historians and biographers been able to get close to the truth about her amazing life and career.

One thing is clear, though: Through talent and hard work, Annie rose from a childhood of poverty and abuse to become one of the modern world's first international superstars.

chapter 1

Struggling Along in Ohio

In the spring of 1855, Jacob and Susan Moses and their three young daughters set out from Pennsylvania for Darke County, Ohio. There they settled on the outskirts of a tiny village called Woodland. The name suited the place. This part of Ohio, right on the state's border with Indiana to the west, was a region of rolling hills and thick forest. Jacob's first job upon arriving in Darke County was to cut down trees to build a log cabin for the family to live in.

In Pennsylvania, the Moses family had barely made a living by running an inn (an establishment that served as a

This log cabin in the hill country of western Ohio is similar to the one in which Annie lived as a young child.

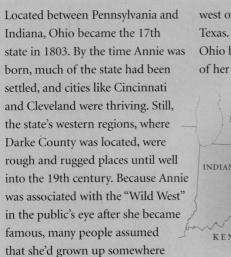

Ohio

Located between Pennsylvania and Indiana, Ohio became the 17th state in 1803. By the time Annie was born, much of the state had been settled, and cities like Cincinnati and Cleveland were thriving. Still, the state's western regions, where Darke County was located, were rough and rugged places until well into the 19th century. Because Annie was associated with the "Wild West" in the public's eye after she became famous, many people assumed that she'd grown up somewhere west of the Mississippi River, like Texas. Annie, however, never hid her Ohio heritage and remained proud of her home state for her entire life.

restaurant and hotel for travelers). But the inn burned down in a fire, leaving Jacob and Susan without jobs, and the family without a home. So, like many Americans in the mid-19th century, the Moses family moved westward. Their goal, like most pioneers of the time, was to farm their own land and lead an independent life.

With hard work, and luck, the land would produce most of the things a pioneer family needed. After the fields were cleared for planting, crops of corn, wheat, and vegetables provided food, along with some pigs, cows, and chickens. The nearby forest yielded nuts, berries, and wood for the fireplace, plus game like deer and wild turkey for the family's table. If all went well, a family could sell some of their

The rolling hills of western Ohio—which Annie knew well from her childhood—become ablaze with color in the fall.

produce in town in order to buy the few things—such as sugar, coffee, and cloth—that they couldn't grow or make themselves. It was a hard life, though. Everyone in the family—even young children—had to help out.

The Moses family grew. On August 13, 1860, a new daughter arrived. She was named Phoebe Ann, but she would always be known as Annie. (It seems that her older sisters thought that Phoebe was too "fancy" a name.) A brother, John, was born in 1862, and another sister, Hulda, arrived two years later.

Annie grew into a little girl with a thick head of dark hair and eyes the color of steel. She wasn't a big child. Even as an adult, she never stood taller than about five feet (1.5 m) or weighed more than about 110 pounds (50 kg). But she was strong and sturdy.

While Annie dutifully helped her mother with household chores in the kitchen and garden, her real love, even at an early age, was the outdoors. Her sisters preferred to stay around the cabin and play with dolls, but Annie liked nothing better than to roam the fields and forests with her father. As she later wrote, "God intended women to be outside as well as men, and they do not know what they are missing when they stay cooped up in the house." From Jacob, Annie learned how to make simple traps—baited with a few kernels of corn—to catch rabbits, squirrels, and birds for food.

Tragedy struck the family in the winter of 1866, when Annie was five and a half years old. One cold December day, Jacob went into town to

Quakers

Annie's parents were Quakers—members of a Christian group called the Society of Friends, which developed in 17th-century England. Quaker worship is simple, and members are expected to dress and speak with modesty and plainness. Quakers are also pacifists—they refuse to take part in war, or to possess weapons. On the frontier in the 19th century, however, Quaker pioneers like Jacob Moses had little choice but to use guns to hunt food for their families.

sell some grain and pick up some supplies. While he was gone, a blizzard set in. As the wind howled and the snow swirled around the cabin, the family waited anxiously for his return. Finally, in the middle of the night, Jacob's horse-drawn wagon came in sight.

Jacob was barely alive. Annie would later recall seeing her father "with the reins around his neck and wrists, for his dear hands had been frozen so he could not use them. His speech was gone." The ordeal was too much for Jacob. He died a few weeks later.

The loss of their father and husband was a huge blow to the Moses family—and not just emotionally. Without Jacob's labor, the family couldn't make a living from their land. First, Susan had to sell the family's cow, named Pink, to pay the bills. Annie and her brothers and sisters loved the animal and cried when it was led away. Then Susan had to sell their farm and move the family to a smaller, rented property.

The next few years were a time of struggle as Annie's mother tried to provide for the family, which by now included seven children. Although Susan took a job as a nurse, the money didn't go very far. "But every night," Annie later recalled, "no matter how tired we were, mother washed our hands and feet, brushed and plaited our hair into pigtails, took little John and Baby Huldie onto her lap . . . and prayed God to watch over us."

This .54-caliber Kentucky rifle is similar to the one that Annie inherited from her father.

When she was seven or eight years old, Annie hit upon a way to help the family. Later in life, Annie told several different versions of the story of how she held a gun in her hands for the first time. In one version, she said that she spotted a squirrel nibbling a nut on a fence outside the cabin and decided to shoot it. She took the long-barreled rifle her father had brought from Pennsylvania to Ohio from above the cabin's fireplace, loaded it, and prepared to fire.

Jacob's rifle was probably a .40 or .50 caliber weapon, which meant it could fire a round lead bullet (often called a ball in those days) about half an inch (1.3 cm) in size. The rifle was a muzzle-loading gun. To load it, Annie would have poured a charge of gunpowder into the mouth (muzzle) of the barrel, followed by a wad of paper or leather, and then the bullet. Then she had to use a long tool called a ramrod to drive the wad and bullet down into the barrel so that they sat firmly on top of the gunpowder. Considering that rifles like this often had barrels up to four feet (1.2m) in length—probably taller than Annie was at the time—this must have been quite a job.

In Annie's time, as today, gray squirrels were a common sight in the eastern half of the United States.

Next, Annie had to put a percussion cap into the lock (the mechanism that

Rifle

A rifle is a type of gun with spiral grooves cut into the inside of the barrel. The grooves cause the bullet to spin in flight, making rifles more accurate than "smooth-bore" guns like muskets and shotguns. German immigrant craftsmen brought the skill of rifle-making to Pennsylvania and other American colonies in the 17th and 18th centuries. It's likely that Jacob's rifle was a "Kentucky rifle" produced by one of these gun makers.

fires the gun). The cap was a tiny metal container filled with an explosive compound. Then she had to pull back the lock's hammer, which cocked the gun—making it ready to fire. When the trigger was pulled, the hammer would hit the percussion cap, which would explode, sending flame through a tiny hole connecting the lock to the inside of the barrel. This would set off the main powder charge, sending the bullet flying toward the target.

Annie recalled that she had "stuffed in enough powder to kill off a buffalo." She rested the long gun on the railing of the cabin's porch and pulled the trigger. When the smoke cleared, the squirrel lay dead, shot cleanly through the head. "I still consider it one of the best shots I ever made," Annie said decades later, when she was world-famous for her shooting.

This was the beginning of Annie's career as a hunter and sharpshooter.

Annie's family wasn't happy with her new hobby, even though it put food on the table. "My mother," Annie later wrote, "was perfectly horrified when I began shooting . . .

but I would run away and go quail shooting in the woods."
Her brother John was angry, too. Girls weren't supposed to
shoot and hunt! One story has it that John tried to frighten
his sister out of her love of shooting by putting an extra load
of gunpowder into his own shotgun and giving it to Annie
to shoot. It seems he hoped the "kick" of the gun against her
shoulder would knock her over and hopefully make his sister
think twice about picking up a gun again. But Annie proved
undaunted by the trick.

In the 1860s, girls were expected to spend their childhoods
preparing for lives as wives and mothers. These were the only
roles open to most women in 19th-century America. At the
time, few jobs besides teaching were considered appropriate
for women. In most of the country, women didn't have the
right to vote or to serve on juries. In the eyes of the law,
women were practically considered the "property" of their
fathers or husbands.

Slowly, though, things were starting to change for American
women. In 1848, a group of
men and women had
gathered in Seneca Falls,
New York, and issued
a "Declaration of
Sentiments" calling

This statue in Seneca Falls,
New York, memorializes
pioneers of the American
women's rights movement.

for greater rights for women. Around the time Annie took her father's gun down from over the fireplace, women like Susan B. Anthony began campaigning for women's right to vote and for more equality between the sexes. And in 1869, the Territory of Wyoming did something that shocked many Americans—it gave women the vote.

Susan B. Anthony risked jail (and was widely ridiculed) in her efforts to gain the vote for American women.

Young Annie knew nothing of these developments. She just knew that she was good at shooting, even though that skill was supposed to be for men and boys only. The ability to handle a gun seemed to come to her naturally.

"Somehow we managed to struggle along for several years" after Jacob's death, Annie later wrote. But by 1870 Susan Moses could no longer hold her family together. Things had gone from bad to worse since Jacob had died. In the ensuing years, one of Annie's older sisters had also died, of tuberculosis. The family had grown so poor that Susan sent Hulda to live with a neighboring family. (In a time with little or no government help for struggling families, this was a common practice.) Things looked up for a bit when Susan remarried, but her new husband died not

TUBERCULOSIS

Tuberculosis is a disease of the lungs that affected many people in the 19th century. While it often took many years to kill its victims, it was almost always fatal.

long afterward. This plunged the family (which included a new child, Emily) into poverty once again.

When Annie was about 10 years old, Susan decided she had no choice but to send her to live at the Darke County Infirmary in Greenville.

Run by the county government, the infirmary took in people who couldn't take care of themselves. Its residents, or "inmates," included children whose parents had died or couldn't feed and house them, as well as mentally and physically handicapped people of all ages.

It's heartbreaking to consider what Annie must have thought when she laid eyes on the grim, three-story brick building. Her life had been hard for as long as she could remember, but at least she'd been part of a loving family. Now she was alone in a terrifying place.

And things were about to get even worse for Annie.

This sentimental 19th-century photograph depicts a young woman dying of tuberculosis— a disease that killed two of Annie's sisters.

chapter 2

Among the Wolves

Not long after Annie arrived at the infirmary, a local farmer showed up looking for a young girl to help his wife—who had just had a baby—with household chores. In return, the farmer promised to give the girl an education and to send money to her family. Annie's mother gave her permission to move in with the couple. When Annie told the farmer of her love for hunting and trapping, he told her she'd have plenty of free time to spend in the woods. It seemed like a good deal for everyone involved.

Annie soon learned that the farmer and his wife were, as she put it, "wolves in sheep's clothing." She never revealed the couple's name in her

Before the advent of modern machinery, farmers had to use horse-driven plows, as shown in this photo from 1886.

writings as a grown-up or in interviews with reporters curious about her early life. To Annie, the couple would always be "the wolves."

This illustration shows the work that had to be done— by all family members— on a 19th-century farm.

The farmer and his wife treated Annie more like a slave than as a household helper. Later, she described a typical day on their farm: "I got up at 4 o'clock in the morning, got breakfast, milked the cows, washed dishes, skimmed milk, fed the calves and pigs, pumped water for the cattle, fed the chickens, rocked the baby to sleep, weeded the garden, picked wild blackberries and got dinner." There certainly wasn't any time for trapping and hunting.

Working for the wolves made Annie so tired that sometimes she fell asleep in the evenings before her work was done. When this happened on one cold winter night, Mrs. Wolf got so angry that she threw Annie out the door and into the snow. Annie thought she was going to die. She must have remembered the terrible sight of her father arriving at the family's cabin, frozen nearly to death. "[I] got down on my my little knees . . . and tried to pray," Annie recalled later, "but my lips were frozen stiff and there was no sound." She was saved only by the appearance of Mr. Wolf. Worried that he'd be angry at her for putting the life of their near-slave in

Annie's first train ride occurred when she fled from the wolves in 1872. She would later spend much of her adult life on trains.

danger, Mrs. Wolf pulled Annie into the warm farmhouse.

The wolves also made no effort to send Annie to school or to teach her to read and write, as they'd promised. And although Annie didn't know it, the wolves were lying to her mother. They sent Susan Moses regular letters saying how well Annie was doing with her schoolwork and how much she liked living with them. Still, Annie's mother may have sensed that something was wrong, because according to some sources, she wrote the wolves asking them to send Annie home. But the wolves refused to let her go. "I was held a prisoner," Annie recalled.

Needless to say, Annie was lonely, scared, and miserable. Besides overworking her, the wolves probably beat Annie, too, although she never liked to talk about this part of her ordeal.

In 1872, when she was 12, Annie couldn't take it anymore. "One fine spring day," in her words, she was ironing some clothes when she noticed the wolf family had left the house. Gathering her few belongings, she locked the door behind her and set out for the nearest train station. There she boarded a train that would take her to a stop close to her mother's new home in North Star, near Woodland. Unfortunately, Annie had only 48 cents—not enough to buy a ticket. A kindly man paid her fare. Annie never forgot this, saying that for years "I prayed to God each night to keep the good man who helped me to get away from the wolves."

Annie still had to walk many miles before she was reunited with her mother. Susan Moses had married again, and Annie liked her new stepfather. But there were problems at home. Susan and her new husband both suffered from poor health, and the family was still struggling to make ends meet.

So Annie returned to the Darke County Infirmary once again. There, she lived with the couple that ran the place—Samuel and Nancy Edington. The Edingtons were kind people, and they treated Annie like one of their own children. They were horrified to hear about how the

The Darke County Infirmary was a sad place, but Annie found some happiness there.

wolves had treated Annie, and they gasped when they saw the scars from the beatings she'd received. When Mr. Wolf showed up at the infirmary demanding that Annie return to the wolves' home, Mr. Edington and his son drove him away and told him never to come back. For the first time in years, Annie felt safe.

While living with the Edingtons, Annie finally learned to read and write. There were lessons in the infirmary's school, and every night Annie was present when the Edington family read aloud to each other for half an hour.

Nancy Edington also taught Annie how to sew, knit, and embroider. These were important skills in an era in which women were expected to make and repair their family's clothes. Even after she became a superstar, Annie continued to work on her own costumes. In fact, her skill with a sewing machine and with embroidery needles was second only to her skill with a rifle, pistol, or shotgun. Embroidery also helped pass the time between shows or traveling between towns.

Annie later described her years with the Edingtons as "happy." Nancy Edington said she sensed that Annie was grown up beyond her years, and that she would be "a great woman if given the chance." Annie certainly proved her worth around the infirmary. Besides sewing clothes for the children, she managed the infirmary's dairy and made

EMBROIDERY

Embroidery is the art of decorating fabric with designs stitched in thread or yarn.

sure that each child got a glass
of milk every day.

Sewing was considered an important skill for girls, as shown in these pictures from a 19th-century children's book.

The Edingtons also put Annie
in charge of the infirmary's storage room. It was a big
responsibility: She had to keep track of important supplies
and make sure the Edingtons knew when to order more.
Annie would later recall sitting "by a kerosene light till
midnight, listing all the things we needed. It was a big
job for so young a girl and my heart thumped for fear
I could not do it." But she did it well. After a while she
felt confident enough to ask the Edingtons to buy some
colorful fabric. It wasn't for her: She'd decided to make
special cuffs and collars to liven up the otherwise drab
uniforms the infirmary's inmates wore.

Annie spent about three years living with the Edingtons
at the infirmary. Her time there had a big influence on
her adult personality. Although she'd had a very hard
childhood, in the infirmary she lived among people whose
lives were even harder. When she won fame and money,
Annie gave generously to charities—especially those that
made children's lives better. And she would often give

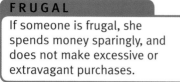

FRUGAL

If someone is frugal, she spends money sparingly, and does not make excessive or extravagant purchases.

children (especially orphans) free tickets to her shows and buy them treats like ice cream afterward.

Also, Annie's early experience of poverty made her very aware of the value of money. She would always be careful with her finances, and she gained a well-deserved reputation as a good businesswoman. Later, some people would describe Annie as being "cheap," but this was mean-spirited. It's certainly true that Annie was very frugal, in contrast with the free-spending ways of other show-business people. But Annie always had to depend on her own earnings, and she knew that without money in the bank, poverty loomed.

When she was about 15, Annie decided that the time had come for her to leave the infirmary. She wanted to be back with her mother, her new stepfather, and her brothers and sisters. She also missed the life she'd known before she came to the infirmary, when she'd trapped and hunted in the woods around her family's farm. "I was homesick for the fairy places," she later wrote, "the green moss, the big toadstools, the wild flowers, the bees . . . the baby rabbits, the squirrels, and the quail."

Before leaving Greenville, Annie stopped in at a store owned by two brothers, G. Anthony and Charles Katzenberger. Their business was typical of the "general stores" found in most small American communities of the time, which got their name from the fact they sold all kinds of merchandise—from groceries to hardware. Annie had probably been to the store many times before to buy supplies for the infirmary.

The Katzenberger brothers also bought game like deer, quail, and rabbit from local huners. They sold some of the game to local residents and shipped the rest to hotels and restaurants in bigger towns, including Cincinnati. Annie asked the Katzenbergers if they'd be willing to buy the game she intended to hunt when she returned home. This was certainly the first time a teenage girl had proposed such an arrangement. But the Katzenbergers knew of Annie's reputation as a good shot, and they agreed.

In the words of one of Annie's biographers, "For the rest of her life she would earn her living with a gun."

This photo shows downtown Greenville, Ohio, in the late 19th century. The town prospered thanks to its location at the junction of three railroad lines.

chapter 3

"I Glided Swiftly through the Woods"

Finally home for good, the teenage Annie roamed the woods around North Star, clad in a woolen dress and carrying a shotgun, stalking rabbit, grouse, and quail. Her natural skill for shooting only improved with practice, especially because she liked to shoot animals and birds when they were in motion, instead of just sitting on the ground or in a tree. To Annie, the woods were paradise: "Oh, how grand God's beautiful earth seems to me as I glided swiftly through the woods," she later wrote.

Annie's mother's house in North Star, Ohio. Money from sales of Annie's game helped pay the mortgage.

Some of the game Annie shot wound up on the family's table. The rest went to the Katzenbergers' store. The money Annie's game brought in was enough to pay off the mortgage on Annie's mother's house. If Annie hadn't earned the $200 needed to repay the bank, the family might have lost their home. As Annie later put it, "my heart leaped with joy as I handed the money to my mother."

According to some stories, the Katzenbergers' customers soon began asking specifically for birds and other game shot by Annie. The reason for this was that Annie was such a good shot that she brought down birds and rabbits with a clean shot through the head, instead of through the body. This way,

Annie as a teenager, with shotgun and rabbit, wearing the type of practical clothing she favored for hunting.

diners wouldn't crack their teeth on a piece of buckshot.

When Annie became famous, people wondered how she had developed her amazing skill with a gun. "I don't know how I acquired the skill . . ." she once said. "I suppose I was born with it." For Annie, nothing was simpler than hitting a target, whether it was a playing card, a clay ball, or a bird on the wing. Later, when she gave shooting lessons, she told her students, "You must have your mind, your nerve, and

29

A shotgun shell with buckshot. The invention of one-piece shells was a big improvement over the old system.

everything in harmony. Don't look at your gun, simply follow [the target] with the end of it, as if the tip of the barrel was the point of your finger."

The Katzenbergers were so happy with Annie's work that they gave her a new shotgun from Parker Brothers, one of the country's finest gun makers. The new gun was a big improvement over the old shotgun that Annie had been using.

The old gun was a muzzle-loader. As we've seen, this meant that before taking a shot, Annie had to pour a measure of gunpowder down the gun's barrel, followed by a wad of paper or leather, and then a charge of buckshot, all of which were rammed into the gun with the ramrod.

The Parker Brothers' gun, however, was an up-to-date breech-loader. Instead of requiring the shooter to load powder, wad, buckshot, and cap separately, it fired a newly invented shotgun shell that combined all of these elements in one piece. Annie only had to put one of these shells in the gun's breech, or rear, and she was ready to shoot.

With her new gun, Annie brought in even more game. "Every mail day," she later wrote, "I sent hampers [baskets] of quail done up in bunches

SHOTGUN

A shotgun is a smooth-bore weapon that fires pellets known as buckshot. It is less accurate than a rifle, but good for shooting game at close range.

of sixes or twelves" to the Katzenbergers. Still, she wasn't a "game hog," as she put it. Her goal wasn't to shoot every bird and animal she came across. In this, Annie was ahead of her time. Today, there are restrictions on the number and kind of game that hunters can shoot, and in most places hunting is restricted to certain times of the year.

When Annie was hunting, however, there were few such laws. As a result, some kinds of birds and animals practically disappeared from parts of the country because of overhunting.

A good example of this is the passenger pigeon. These birds once numbered in the billions. But in the last decades of the 19th century, the birds were trapped and hunted to extinction. By 1900, they had disappeared from the skies. The last living passenger pigeon died in a zoo in 1914.

The great naturalist John James Audubon made this print of the passenger pigeon decades before it became extinct.

While Annie earned a reputation among her neighbors as a crack shot, target shooting was becoming a major sport in America—almost as popular as baseball, football, and basketball are today. Thousands of people flocked to shooting ranges to watch "exhibition" shooters fire at paper targets or blast glass balls out of the air.

Gauge and Caliber

Shotguns are classified by gauge, a measurement that combines the width of the gun's barrel and the amount of buckshot pellets that could fit into it, expressed as fractions of a pound. Rifles and pistols are classified by caliber, the width of the barrel as expressed as fractions of an inch. The higher the caliber, the bigger the bullet the gun is designed to fire.

The top marksmen—like W. F. "Doc" Carver and Adam Bogardus—were big celebrities. Bogardus became famous when, in 1869, he shot 100 pigeons in a row, missing none. This was an example of trap shooting, in which live birds (usually pigeons) were released from cages to serve as targets. (Eventually, clay disks hurled by spring-loaded machines replaced live birds. The disks became known as "clay pigeons.") Nine years later, Doc Carver amazed fans of exhibition shooting by shattering 5,500 out of 6,208 glass balls in more than eight hours of nonstop shooting.

Target shooting was an international sport, too. In 1874, when an American rifle team beat the top-ranked Irish team in a match at Creedmoor, Long Island, not far from New York City, the news made headlines across the country.

Changes in gun technology made these events exciting for spectators. Before about 1860, almost all guns could fire only one shot before being reloaded. Around the time of the Civil War (1861–65), however, gun makers developed "repeating rifles" that could fire several times without reloading. Depending on the type of gun, the magazine could hold between seven and fifteen cartridges, which an experienced shooter could empty in almost as many seconds.

"Trick" or "fancy" shooting was also popular. Usually working in two-man teams, trick shooters entertained theater audiences by shooting pieces of fruit or potatoes out of one another's hands or off their heads, shooting out candle flames, and blasting the corks out of bottles. Trick shooters also delighted spectators with stunts like shooting with their guns pointed backward over their shoulders, using mirrors to aim.

Shooting wasn't just a spectator sport. In the decades after the Civil War, shooting enthusiasts formed gun clubs and eagerly competed against one another. Trap-shooting, rifle, and pistol ranges sprang up in many communities. Out in the countryside, marksmen competed in "turkey shoots," with a plump bird as the prize. It's said that Annie took part in such competitions in Darke County—until the local men banned her. She was just too good.

This advertising card depicts Annie, Buffalo Bill, Adam Bogardus, and Doc Carver as "world champions" of shooting.

In 1881, however, Annie entered a shooting match that would change her life forever.

4

Butler & Oakley

One "trick shot" of the time was a handsome, dark-haired young man named Frank Butler. Born in Ireland around 1850, he came to America by himself when he was just 13. In New York City, he worked odd jobs and, for a time, made his living as a fisherman. Then he drifted into show business as the manager of a team of trained dogs.

This photograph of Frank Butler was taken around 1883, not long after he and Annie were married.

Witty and charming, Frank was a fine storyteller. One of his favorite tales described how his dog act came to a sudden end during a performance in Philadelphia. The leading dog had spent his early life as a fire dog accompanying firemen as they put out blazes. The Philadelphia theater happened to be next door to a firehouse. When the fire alarm rang, the lead dog leaped off the stage to join the horse-drawn fire engines, with the rest of the canine performers following him out the door.

Fortunately for Frank's show-business career, he soon discovered that he had a natural talent for shooting. By the mid-1870s he was traveling around the country with circuses and other traveling shows. One of his tricks was to shoot an apple off the head of his poodle, George.

The spring of 1881 found Frank Butler in Cincinnati, Ohio. With his partner, a man named Baughman, Frank performed a "fancy shooting act" with the Sells Brothers Circus. At his hotel one day, he met some farmers from the countryside who offered to set up a match with an "unknown" shooter near the town of Greenville. The winner would get a prize of $100—a sum equal to about $2,000 today.

As Frank told the story later, he took up the challenge, boasting that the only men who could outshoot him were the famous Adam Bogardus and Doc Carver. He figured

Circuses in the late 19th century were often grand affairs, as shown by this illustration from 1874.

THE GRAND LAY-OUT.

it would be easy money. He was a professional. How hard could it be to outshoot some farm boy or backwoods hunter? In Frank's words, "It seemed like a shame for me to take the money from these country people. . . . [But] as I needed it I went out."

Greenville was 80 miles (129 km) from Cincinnati, and it wasn't easy to get to. He'd have to walk 18 miles (29 km) from the nearest train station. When Frank showed up for the match after his long hike along a muddy country road, he found "most of the county" waiting for the match to begin, as he told a writer many years later. He was in for the surprise of his life. "You may bet . . . that I almost dropped dead when a little slim girl . . . stepped up to the mark with me."

It was Annie. Was she nervous? We don't know for sure, but she well might have been. Like Frank, Annie was confident in her ability with a gun. Before this

This newspaper illustration shows a typical trap-shooting competition. The man behind the shooter is pulling a string to release a bird from the trap.

In addition to being part of his act, Frank's poodle, George, acted as a "go-between" during his romance with Annie.

fateful day, though, she'd done most of her shooting by herself, in the woods. She might have tested her skills against local marksmen in turkey shoots, but this was the first time she'd ever competed against a professional shooter with a big cash prize at stake.

The match was a trap-shooting competition using live pigeons. Frank and Annie each had 25 birds to shoot. When the sound of the last gunshots died away, Annie had downed 23 birds to Frank's 21. It was the first time Frank Butler had ever lost a match.

Frank found himself attracted to the "little slim girl" who'd outshot him. (In fact, the little girl was about twenty years old.) "Right then and there," he later said, "I decided that if I could get that girl I would do it." He invited Annie and her family to see his act in Cincinnati. When Frank performed his signature trick of shooting an apple off George's head, the dog went into the audience and laid a piece of the shattered fruit at Annie's feet.

After Frank went back on the road, the two sent each other letters and gifts. Perhaps because of her shy nature, Annie pretended to write her letters to George, rather than Frank. Getting into the spirit of things, Frank did the same with his letters to Annie. He also sent Annie a poem expressing his feelings for her:

There's a charming little girl
She's many miles from here
She's a loving little fairy
You'd fall in love to see her
Her presence would remind you
Of an angel in the skies,
And you bet I love this little girl
With the rain drops in her eyes.

Just how Annie felt about Frank at first isn't really known. They were opposites in many ways. Frank had an outgoing nature and he had seen a lot of the world. Annie was modest and shy, and she'd hardly been out of Darke County. And if Annie had ever been romantically involved with a man before she met Frank, there's no record of it.

On the other hand, they had some things in common. Both Annie and Frank had known poverty and hardship, and they both made their own way in the world from an early age.

This poster portrays some of the trick shots Frank and his partner performed in their act.

It may also be that Annie's mother and other family members didn't look kindly toward Frank, at least at the start of their relationship. There was the 10-year age difference, for one thing. Worse perhaps, in their eyes, was the fact that Frank had been married before and was now divorced. Divorce was rare at the time and considered immoral by many people. Given their Quaker heritage, Annie's family might also have been worried about Frank's

A studio portrait shows Annie's romantic side, as she poses with flowers instead of her usual firearm.

involvement in show business. (Professional performers were often regarded with some suspicion during this era.)

Still, Annie's family understood that Frank was an honest, hard-working, and clean-living man—he didn't drink alcohol, smoke, or gamble, and he was just as aware of the value of a dollar earned as Annie was. And he clearly was head-over-heels in love with her.

Regardless of how their relationship developed, Frank and Annie got married a year or so after they met. The exact date and place of the wedding isn't certain, but it probably took place in 1882, perhaps in Canada.

By then Frank had quit the Sells Brothers Circus and was touring with a new partner, John Graham. Billing themselves as "America's rifle team and champion all-around shots," they specialized in indoor trick shooting, and Frank's trademark stunt involved shooting while bending over backward.

Little is known about how Annie spent the first months of her marriage to Frank. She may have stayed at home in Ohio with her family most of the time while Frank was performing. But she was with him on May 1, 1882, when Butler & Graham were scheduled to appear at Crystal Hall in Springfield, Ohio.

John Graham fell ill. In need of a partner, Frank brought Annie on stage. "I went on," she wrote later, "with Mr. B. to hold the objects as he shot . . . But I rebelled." Annie decided to take some shots herself. (Another story about that night has it that a man in the audience encouraged Annie by shouting, "Let the girl shoot!" when Frank missed several shots.)

When Annie started shooting, the crowd went wild. There was something appealing about the sight of this small, young woman hefting a big gun and knocking down target after target, rarely missing. When she left the stage, she kicked her foot backward toward the audience. This girlish action would become one of her signature moves for the rest of her career.

Frank and Annie realized they had a hit on their hands. Soon, they worked up their own team act. There was never any doubt, though, about who was the better shot. In Frank's words, "I didn't teach her how to shoot, because she could have taught me even then, although I was supposed to be a crack shot in those days. I simply got her a position and she did the rest."

Still, it was Frank who showed Annie how to do the trick shots that audiences loved. Shooting on a theater stage was a lot different than bringing down quail in the forests of rural Ohio. For one thing, electric light bulbs had just been invented, and most theaters were still lit by smoky gas lights that made it hard to see the targets.

The couple performed under the name "Butler & Oakley." Annie had a new last name to go along with her new career as a performer. It seems she never liked the last name "Moses." Sometimes she insisted on spelling it "Mozee." Now, she decided that "Oakley" would be her last name. No one is sure why. There was a town near Cincinnati by that name; maybe Annie just liked the sound of it. Others think "Oakley" may have been the last name of the kindly man who'd paid her train fare when she escaped from the wolves many years before. In any case, Annie Moses would now be Annie Oakley.

One of the first publicity photos of the husband-and-wife team of Butler & Oakley—with George at their feet.

chapter 5

Sitting Bull and the Circus

The next few years were hard but happy ones for Frank and Annie. They performed in theaters, concert halls, and skating rinks, staying in cheap hotels or trying to sleep in hard-backed seats on trains as they traveled from town to town. But they had each other for company, as well as George the poodle, who went everywhere with them and was part of their act. When they weren't traveling, they visited Annie's mother in Ohio.

Butler & Oakley were part of a huge army of performers who crisscrossed America in the last decades of the 19th century. This was a time when entertainment meant live entertainment. "Moving pictures"—the movies—and the radio came on the scene in the 1890s, but it would be years before they became part of most people's lives. Television and the Internet were far in the future.

So Americans who wanted to escape from the cares of their everyday lives for a few hours went

General Tom Thumb, who stood 25 inches (65 cm) tall, was a major attraction in showman P. T. Barnum's circus.

Exotic animals were another feature of traveling shows and circuses, as shown by this poster from 1880.

to plays, concerts, operas, and after around 1881, the new "vaudeville" theaters that sprang up in every American town of any size. For a few cents admission, vaudeville offered audiences a wide variety of entertainment in a single show—dancers and acrobats, singers and comedians, trained animals and magicians. Vaudeville shows often also included appearances by celebrities of the day, as well as short plays—and shooting acts like Butler & Oakley.

Along with vaudeville, this era was also the heyday of traveling circuses, which had many of the same acts, plus exotic animals—including elephants, rhinoceroses, and hippopotamuses—"freak shows," and other attractions. These circuses and other traveling shows owed much of their success to the rise of the railroad in America. Between 1860 and the early 1880s, the amount of railroad tracks in the United States had more than tripled, making it possible for big shows to visit many cities, towns, and villages in a single season. These circuses traveled on special trains and performed under a huge canvas tent—the "big top." In 1884, the Sells Brothers Circus (whose trains carried no fewer than 50 cages of wild animals) appeared in almost 200 communities and traveled more than 10,000 miles (16,000 km).

In their first years as an act, Butler & Oakley sometimes performed on their own and sometimes joined traveling troupes of entertainers. They were still little known.

In 1884, however, Annie crossed paths with someone who was very famous indeed. That person was Sitting Bull, a leader of the Sioux, or Lakota, nation of American Indians. The meeting would help launch her on the way to worldwide fame.

In the years after the Civil War, white settlers and railroad builders had pushed westward into the vast grasslands of

Sitting Bull, as he appeared around 1888, photographed in a studio in Bismarck, in what was then the Dakota Territory.

A romanticized depiction of the Battle of Little Bighorn—a fight that also became known as "Custer's Last Stand."

the Great Plains—a region that was the homeland of Indian nations such as the Sioux, the Cheyenne, and the Arapaho. In the mid-1870s, gold was discovered in the Black Hills of the Dakota Territory (now the states of North and South Dakota). This was land guaranteed to the Indians by a treaty with the United States government. But when the Indians resisted the invasion of their land, the government sent in the army.

In June 1876, warriors led by Sitting Bull and another Sioux leader, Crazy Horse, wiped out all 268 men of a cavalry unit led by a famous officer, Lieutenant Colonel George Custer, along the banks of the Little Bighorn River in what is now the state of Montana. The Indian victory shocked many white Americans. The army sent in more troops. Sitting Bull and some of his people fled to Canada, but a few years later they returned to American territory and accepted life on a reservation.

Sitting Bull

In the Lakota language, the name "Sitting Bull" (Tatanka Iyotanka) really means something like "the male buffalo that refuses to move." It was a fitting name for a man who spent his life trying to defend his people, their way of life, and their homeland. Born around 1831, Sitting Bull became a major Sioux chief in the 1860s. While white Americans considered him a warrior chief, Sitting Bull was really more of a religious leader. He died in 1890, killed in his home on a Sioux reservation by police who thought he was about to lead an uprising.

Officially, Sitting Bull was a prisoner, but he was allowed to travel occasionally under the control of a government agent. The federal government's Office of Indian Affairs hoped that once he'd seen "civilization," Sitting Bull would encourage his people to put aside their traditional ways and become more like white Americans—by taking up farming, for example. Sitting Bull was impressed by some of things he saw—like the telephone. But he also noted the gap between the rich and the poor in the cities he visited. This contrasted with American Indian society, where people shared what they had, so that if hunting was good, no one went hungry.

Sitting Bull created a sensation whenever he visited a city. The same white Americans who had called him a "murderer" after Custer's defeat now lined up eagerly to get a look at the famous American Indian leader. Sitting Bull used these appearances as a way to earn money by selling autographed pictures of himself to the curious crowds. He would then use the money to help his people, who were struggling in poverty on their reservation.

In March 1884, Sitting Bull was in St. Paul, Minnesota. So were Frank and Annie, performing as an act in a troupe called the Arlington & Fields Combination. On the night of March 19, Sitting Bull sat in the audience at St. Paul when Annie and Frank did their act. The warrior chief looked on in fascination as Annie knocked the targets down.

After the show, Sitting Bull sent a messenger to Frank and Annie's hotel, asking for a meeting. At first, Annie turned the chief down. She was very tired. In addition to their theater act, she'd been shooting in local target competitions to bring in much-needed cash. But Sitting Bull wouldn't take no for an answer. He sent another messenger, this time

This Christmas card proudly displays the nickname given to Annie by her friend Sitting Bull.

offering $65 in return for a meeting. Annie sent back the money and agreed to see the chief the next day.

When they met, Sitting Bull gave Annie a new nickname—Watanya Cecila, which meant "Little Sure Shot" in Lakota, the Sioux language. Besides his admiration for Annie's shooting, Sitting Bull was struck by how much she looked like his own daughter, who had died years earlier. The chief gave

This Sells Brothers circus poster dates from around the time Frank and Annie performed with the show.

her several presents, including the moccasins he'd worn at the Little Bighorn fight. Later, a legend would spring up that Sitting Bull had officially adopted "Little Sure Shot" as a daughter. There's no proof of this, but the two certainly became friends.

Frank quickly saw that Annie's meeting with Sitting Bull could be used to gain attention for their act. He placed an advertisement in a New York City newspaper proclaiming that "the premier shots, Butler and Oakley" had been "captured" by Sitting Bull.

The act's fame was growing, but Frank and Annie were still struggling to make a living. Not long after the meeting with Sitting Bull, the pair joined the Sells Brothers Circus, the outfit Frank had been working for when they first met.

Traveling with Sells Brothers provided a steady paycheck, but it seems Frank and Annie weren't very happy with the organization. For one thing, Annie felt that the circus didn't treat its human and animal performers very well. For another, Annie and Frank weren't typical show-business people. At the time, traveling entertainers had a reputation (deserved or not) for loose morals. "Show people" were supposed to like drinking, smoking, and gambling, and to spend every dollar they earned even before it was in their pocket.

Neither Annie nor Frank had any of these habits, and they were very careful with their money. Annie also held onto the Quaker value of modesty that she'd been brought up with as a young girl in

With her medals and trophies beside her, Annie loads a shell into the breech of a shotgun in this publicity photo.

In this 1885 photo, Buffalo Bill poses with a satin shirt, a pair of Colt revolvers, and a Colt-Burgess lever-action rifle.

Darke County. Throughout her career, she refused suggestions to use makeup, or to wear skimpy outfits that would show more of her body. She wanted to be judged by her shooting skills, not by her appearance.

Still, Annie learned how to connect with her audiences. In fact, her modest manners were a big part of her appeal as a performer. She would hop, skip, and jump onstage, wearing one of her homemade dresses and a pair of thick stockings. If she missed a shot, she would stamp her foot in disappointment. (Often, Annie would miss a few shots on purpose—just to keep the audience's attention.) And she never failed to give a little bow to the spectators before she left the stage.

In December 1884, the Sells Brothers Circus trains puffed into New Orleans, Louisiana. Because they performed outdoors, circuses arranged their schedules so they'd be in the warmer South during the winter months. This winter was especially cold even in the South, though, so the circus ended its run early. This left Frank and Annie without work until the spring.

Frank thought he could find them a new job in the meantime. There was another traveling troupe that was passing through New Orleans—Buffalo Bill's Wild West, which a former army scout and professional hunter, William F. "Buffalo Bill" Cody, had started the previous year. Frank asked Cody to make Butler & Oakley a part of his show.

Sorry, Cody replied. He already had Adam Bogardus, one of America's most famous target shooters, on the payroll. He didn't need any more shooting acts. Besides, there were now several other female shooters performing with various shows, most of them better known than Annie.

Disappointed, Annie and Frank went back north to try to make a living on the vaudeville circuit. Within a few months, however, they got another chance to join up with Buffalo Bill.

This turn-of-the-century view of St. Charles Avenue in New Orleans shows the unique architecture for which the city is known.

chapter 6

The Wild West

When Annie Oakley and William F. Cody first met in 1884, the legendary American "Wild West" was starting to fade into history. There were still plenty of wild, wide-open spaces between the Mississippi River and the shores of the Pacific Ocean, but the frontier—the border between settled and unsettled land in the West—was disappearing. Later, in a famous lecture, historian Frederick Jackson Turner proclaimed that the frontier had finally vanished in the early 1890s.

The vast grasslands of the Great Plains—once home to Native American nations like Sitting Bull's Sioux—were now filling up with farms. (Under the federal government's Homestead Act of 1862, any male

This 1898 painting by Charlie Russell—who was a cowboy as a young man—captures the drama of the Wild West.

"head of household" could claim 640 acres of western land for free if he settled on it for five years.) The era of the great cattle drives—in which cowboys brought thousands

Sioux survivors of the massacre at Wounded Knee huddle in the cold on their South Dakota reservation.

of almost-wild longhorn cattle north from Texas, to towns where they could be sent by railroad to slaughterhouses in cities like Chicago—was ending. The open range of the southern plains was giving way to ranches hemmed in by fences made with a new invention: barbed wire.

The losers in the scramble to settle the West were the land's first people, the American Indians. By the mid-1880s, the Indians—from the Sioux of the northern plains to the Apaches of the Arizona desert—had been defeated by the army and herded onto grim reservations, where they depended on government-supplied food to survive. The last major clash between whites and Indians would come in December 1890, at Wounded Knee, South Dakota—a one-sided fight in which soldiers with cannons massacred more then 150 Sioux men, women, and children.

For other Americans, though, the settling of the West was a grand adventure story. Novels and plays set in the Wild

This romantic depiction of Buffalo Bill was created around 1870, when he was starting his climb to fame.

West became popular decades before the "end of the frontier." These were more fiction than fact, but people in the settled parts of the country loved to hear about cowboys and Indians, scouts and soldiers, gun-slinging bandits and brave lawmen, gamblers and gold seekers.

Naturally, a lot of people tried to make money out of the public's love of anything western. The most successful of these people was William Frederick Cody—a man who had really lived a Wild West life, even if some episodes of his career were exaggerated or made up.

Cody was born in Iowa in 1846, and later moved to Kansas with his family. Like Annie, he lost his father when he was a child and had to go to work to support his family. At 11, Cody helped out on wagon trains heading west. Three years later, he became a rider for the Pony Express, which carried mail on horseback between Missouri and California before the first telegraph line reached the West Coast in 1861.

After fighting for the Union in the Civil War, Cody worked as a hunter for the Kansas Pacific Railroad, shooting buffalo to feed the workers who were laying track across the plains. This gave him his nickname,

"Buffalo Bill." In one eight-month period, he shot more than 4,000 of the animals. Then, in 1868, he became a scout for the army. Although he wasn't officially a solder, his job involved moving ahead of army units in search of Indians. Eventually, he would fight in nine battles against the Indians.

In 1872, when he was 26, Buffalo Bill made his show-business debut. Ned Buntline—famous author of dime novels set in the West—had heard of Cody's adventures and convinced him to appear in a play called *Scouts of the Prairie* in Chicago. By all accounts, the play was terrible, but Cody himself was a hit with audiences. With his long hair, goatee beard, deerskin clothes, and broad-brimmed hat, he seemed the very image of the fearless frontiersman. In the words of Shirl Kasper, a respected biographer of Annie Oakley, "Cody became a symbol for all the best the frontier had to offer—the freedom,

Dime Novels

Around 1860, publishers began selling short books (usually selling for 10 cents) featuring the fictionalized exploits of Western heroes like Kit Carson, Wild Bill Hickock—and of course, Buffalo Bill Cody. By the end of his life, Buffalo Bill had been the subject of no less than 1,700 dime novels.

The Wild West was a true traveling show—everything about it was mobile, including the ticket office.

the excitement, and the heroism."

So the scout and hunter became an actor, although he took time off from the stage to guide hunting parties and work for the army in the West. In 1876, Cody made national headlines when he killed (and scalped) a Cheyenne warrior, Yellow Hair, supposedly in revenge for the death of Custer at Little Bighorn (historians still argue about the facts of this incident).

In the early 1880s Cody went into show business full time. He decided to put together a western-themed traveling show called "Buffalo Bill's Wild West." It would be a show on a scale like no other, with real wild animals, real cowboys, and real Indians, not to mention rodeo and shooting acts. Posters proclaimed that it would give audiences "a visit West in three hours!" The centerpiece was the Attack on the Deadwood Stage, a dramatic version of the historic Indian ambush of a stagecoach traveling between Deadwood, South Dakota, and Cheyenne, Wyoming.

The show first opened to the public in Omaha, Nebraska, in 1883. Over the next 30 years, its worldwide success would end up making Buffalo Bill perhaps the most famous American of his time.

But that was in the future. The show nearly failed in its first couple of years. Paying and transporting all those performers and animals cost a lot of money, and there was plenty of competition from the usual circuses and other traveling shows. The show also suffered from plain bad luck—for example, a boat carrying much of the show's gear sank in the Mississippi River. Also, Cody wasn't very good at handling the business side of the show. By the time Annie and Frank came looking for a job with the Wild West in December 1884, the show was practically broke.

Still, Annie wanted to work for Buffalo Bill. But why would she want to join a show that was deeply in debt, and which still had to prove itself with audiences?

As we've seen, Annie wasn't happy with the Sells Brothers Circus for various reasons. She and Frank were also probably unhappy with many

Buffalo Bill gallantly helps a woman from a stagecoach in his popular "Attack on the Deadwood Stage" act.

of the vaudeville theaters in which they performed on their own. These establishments often appealed to a mostly male audience, sold alcohol during performances, and featured acts that included female dancers in skimpy costumes and comedians who told dirty jokes and stories. All of this made Annie and Frank uncomfortable. In fact, in the early 1880s, they always tried to work at the vaudeville theaters run by New York–based showman Tony Pastor. Unlike many of his competitors, Pastor prided himself on providing wholesome entertainment for the entire family.

Like Tony Pastor, Buffalo Bill Cody and his business manager, Nate Salsbury, put on a "clean" show with family appeal. Cody and Salsbury promoted the Wild West as "America's National Entertainment" and claimed that it was educational as well as entertaining. This must have appealed to Annie, with her strong belief in clean living and traditional values.

Annie probably also wanted to get off the vaudeville circuit

When this photo of Buffalo Bill was taken, in early 1883, the Wild West show was still struggling for success.

because many competing shooting acts were simply cheaters. As historian Louis S. Warren puts it, "Many shooting acts were stage trickery, with candles snuffed out, matches lit, and apples split by hidden devices rather than carefully aimed bullets. . . . [All] shooting acts walked a line between trickery and authentic skill, and audiences wondered at them just as at magic shows and card tricks."

This photo was taken around the time Annie joined the Wild West. The six-pointed star on her hat was a trademark throughout her career.

Annie never cheated, but she may have been stung by the thought that audiences might suspect that she was faking. With the Wild West, she'd be performing not on a dimly lit indoor stage (which made such cheating easier) but in the open air under a canvas tent. That way, no one could suspect that anything other than her amazing skill was at work when she performed.

In early 1885, Adam Bogardus, the Wild West's top shooting act, quit the show. When they heard the news, Annie and Frank asked for another chance to try out. Cody agreed, although he was still wary. For one thing, Annie would have to use shotguns that weighed 10 pounds—and she only weighed 110 pounds herself. Cody, however, might have heard of an amazing feat of "endurance shooting" that Annie

Annie poses with some Indian members of the Wild West, demonstrating her ability to shoot from horseback.

Annie put it, Cody "was the kindest hearted, broadest minded, simplest, most loyal man I ever knew."

Cody quickly saw the wisdom of his partner's decision and made Annie a featured performer in the show. There were a lot of female shooting acts in show business by now, but Annie was clearly different. Most of the other woman shooters relied as much on their appearance—aided by fancy costumes—as on their shooting skills. Annie, as we've seen, refused to make "feminine wiles" part of her act.

What's more, other female shooters generally used rifles to shoot at nonmoving targets such as apples, corks, and candles. While Annie was a crack shot with any kind of firearm, her standard weapon was a shotgun, and she shot at moving targets—usually hard clay balls. She'd toss these up in the air by herself—sometimes two or more at a time—and shatter them into splinters before they hit the ground. It was the kind of shooting she'd learned during her teenage years, bringing down birds on the wing in the woods of Darke County.

Using a shotgun was also a safety measure. Accidentally shooting a paying customer is bad for business, of course. Shotgun pellets don't travel as far as rifle bullets. Buckshot from the shotguns Annie used didn't go much farther than about 180 feet (55 m). Even if she missed, the pellets would just hit the canvas of the big top and fall to the ground. (On occasions when Annie did use a rifle, it's said that windows were broken thousands of feet away.) Some people thought that Annie was cheating by using a shotgun rather than a rifle, but in fact, hitting moving targets with a shotgun at the speed at which Annie shot was just as hard, if not harder, than using a rifle.

In this publicity photo, Annie performs her famous "mirror trick" using a .22 Marlin rifle.

Annie did do plenty of trick shooting in her performances—for example, she would often shoot backward over her shoulder, using a mirror to aim at a target behind her. And after she started with Buffalo Bill's Wild West, she developed a new skill—shooting from horseback, which proved to be a real crowd-pleaser, although it did not become a regular part of her Wild West act. In the end, it was her remarkable accuracy that made the show's audiences gasp in astonishment. Once she hefted her shotgun to her shoulder and began blasting away, no one could doubt that she was the real deal.

chapter 7

The Drama of Civilization

When Annie joined the Wild West the Butler & Oakley act came to an end. Frank traveled along with the show, but he didn't perform. Instead, he settled into the role of Annie's helper and manager. During shows, he operated the launcher that sent clay pigeons into the air and held up targets for Annie to shoot.

Frank never showed any bitterness at being out of the spotlight. Talented as he was, he knew that Annie was the better shot. "She outclassed me," he once said. Frank's willingness to stay in the background was unusual for the time, when husbands were supposed to be the breadwinners and wives were expected to be content with keeping house. But their marriage was a true partnership. The deep bond between them was clear to anyone who met

"The Peerless Wing [shotgun] and Rifle Shot," proclaims this poster, published at the height of Annie's fame.

the couple. From the early 1880s on, they rarely spent a day apart.

Meanwhile, the Wild West's popularity grew, thanks in part to Annie's act, and to the ingenuity of the show's press agent "Arizona John" Burke, who quickly understood Annie's combination of wholesome appeal and natural talent. It was his job to get the press and the public interested in the show, and to help bring in customers. Soon he was spending thousands of dollars to print up and distribute flyers and posters with Annie's picture. Reporters began to take notice of the

Sitting Bull and Buffalo Bill in 1885—the year of the great Sioux leader's one and only tour with the Wild West.

show's female shooting star. A Massachusetts paper marveled when she shattered 55 out of 56 target balls in a row in one performance, noting that "the last [shot] only missed because she tripped over the uneven ground." The *New York Tribune* said that Annie's "finger touch on the trigger" was as precise as the mechanism of a watch.

In June 1885, the show gained a new attraction—none other than Sitting Bull. According to some accounts, the chief refused Cody's request to join the show until he learned that "Little Sure Shot" was part of it. In reality, Sitting Bull

Some of the Wild West's Indian performers relax between shows with a spirited game of Ping-Pong.

probably joined the Wild West because he hoped that by appearing before the public, he could influence the government in Washington to help his people. (Even after he joined, he didn't really perform; he rode in the parade that took place before each performance and appeared before the audience for a few minutes before the show began.) In any case, Annie was delighted to be reunited with Sitting Bull: "He is a dear, faithful, old friend, and I've great respect and affection for him," she wrote.

It may seem strange that Cody was able to recruit Indian performers to join the show. After all, Cody's fame rested on his reputation as an "Indian fighter," and his nickname came from his time slaughtering huge numbers of the animals that the Indians of the Great Plains depended on for survival.

But the Wild West's Indians, who were mostly Sioux, actually got along well with Cody. He treated them with fairness and honesty—and over the years, many great warriors and chiefs joined the show. Also, many of the Wild West's Indians were hard-pressed to support their families on the reservations, and traveling with the show gave them the chance to make money to send home. In the words of one Indian performer, "They told us this show would go across the big water to strange lands, and I thought I ought to go, because I might learn some secret of the Wasichu [white people] that would help my people somehow."

Sitting Bull left the show at the end of the 1885 season. In an interview, the chief said that he missed his family and was "sick of the houses, and the noises" of the white world. He'd also had enough of being a curiosity to audiences. Still, Sitting Bull had friendly feelings toward Cody until his own death— at the hands of reservation police—five years later.

Meanwhile, Annie enjoyed her new career with the Wild West. Still, life on

Buffalo

In the mid-19th century, tens of millions of buffalo (or American bison) roamed the Great Plains. Many Indian tribes depended on the animal, but by the 1880s, white hunters had reduced the population to only a few thousand. Thanks to the efforts of ranchers, there are now 350,000 buffalo in the West.

the road was tough, with the show stopping in one town or city for a few days before packing up and moving on to the next, usually at night. When they weren't aboard the Wild West's train, Annie and Frank lived in a tent cluttered with Annie's guns. At first, they shared a hammock, until Cody gave them some cots—and a portable bathtub.

Annie began the day with a bath, followed by breakfast. Despite her small frame, she had a hearty appetite, and the morning meal often included "good coffee, bread, butter, preserves, fine steaks broiled over wood coals, with fruits and berries in season." In the afternoon, there was target practice. After a nap and another meal, Annie usually spent some time writing letters, and then she was ready for the day's show. When she wanted to relax, or to pass the time spent traveling from town

The Wild West was like a small town on wheels. Here, the troupe lines up for a meal cooked in portable kitchens.

to town, she took up her embroidery needles.

The Wild West troupe included former cowboys, hunters, scouts, and soldiers, and they could be a rowdy bunch. Like their boss, many were fond of drinking and carousing. Annie didn't take part in these activities but she was still popular

Annie reads in a rocking chair outside her tent during the Wild West's run at the Chicago World's Fair of 1893.

with her fellow performers. Some of them teased her because of her thrifty ways, joking that she lived entirely on the free lemonade that Cody made available to the troupe. And while Annie certainly disapproved of drunkenness, it's said she would sometimes join her fellow performers for a glass of beer—as long as someone else was paying.

Indeed, Annie developed longtime friendships with many members of the Wild West. One of her best friends was Johnny Baker, who was just 15 when Annie joined the show in 1884. Billed as "the Cowboy Kid" or the "Boy Marksman," Baker, like Annie, was a crack shot—his signature trick was to fire a rifle while standing on his head. They remained close for the rest of Annie's life, and

CAROUSING

Carousing means to drink heavily and excessively, or to engage in loud and boisterous merrymaking while drunk.

69

An arch welcoming the Wild West to New York City stretched across Broadway when the show came to town.

Baker became something like an adopted son to her.

The Wild West's 1885 season was a triumph. Cody bragged that the show had made more money than any other traveling troupe that year. As for Annie, she was still far from becoming the household name she'd one day be, but her fame was growing.

Annie and Frank were saddened, though, by the death of George the poodle, who got sick and died during an engagement in Ohio. The other performers loved George, too, and his burial was a sorrowful affair—complete with Indian funeral rites.

As the 1886 season opened, the Wild West headed for its biggest challenge yet—New York City.

New York was America's biggest and most cosmopolitan city, and the nation's entertainment capital. Its audiences were famously hard to please. Cody, Annie, and company might have been worried about how the show would be received as they arrived in town. But New York loved the Wild West as much as the rest of the country. Because it was an outdoor spectacle, the show set up not in crowded Manhattan, but on nearby Staten Island. This meant that people from Manhattan,

Brooklyn, and surrounding areas had to take a ferry to see the show. No matter. Some 360,000 people came—28,000 on just one day. They even came on Sundays (the show's one day off) just to look at the animals, the Indians, the Mexican and American cowboys—and Annie.

Annie, however, was upset about a new addition to the show. Cody and his business associates were always looking for new attractions to draw even more people to the Wild West. So, in 1886, they hired another female sharpshooter—a 15-year-old from California named Lillian Smith.

Like Annie, Lillian showed amazing talent with a gun at an early age. She was so good that her father offered $5,000 to anyone who could beat her in a rifle-shooting match—when she was just 10 years old. No one took up the bet.

Annie's teenage rival, Lillian Smith, was guided early in her career by her father, who owned a shooting gallery.

Lillian's specialty was the rifle, and Annie's was the shotgun. Perhaps Cody thought that because they used different weapons, there wouldn't be any jealousy between his two star female shooters. If so, he was wrong.

Even though Lillian used another kind of gun, Annie

viewed the teenager as a rival. Modest as Annie was, she hated being outshone. When the Wild West (Lillian Smith included) began its run on Staten Island with a parade in Manhattan, for example, Annie insisted on taking part—even though she was very sick from an ear infection. And to make herself seem closer in age to Lillian, Annie suddenly changed her birth date so that it appeared that she was only 20, not 26. This was a rare instance of Annie being dishonest—and it led to confusion about her real age for many years.

After four months of sold-out performances on Staten Island, Cody decided to turn the Wild West into an indoor show, which he called "The Drama of Civilization." Playing at Manhattan's Madison Square Garden—the city's most fashionable place of entertainment—the indoor version was also a smash, and it kept Annie and the other performers working throughout the fall and winter. When she wasn't onstage, Annie could often be found competing in shooting contests around New York.

Despite her new fame, Annie still faced prejudice against woman shooters. "It was up-hill work," she recalled. Much of this prejudice came

Madison Square Garden has existed in several versions. This 1890 building was perhaps the most impressive.

not from her male competitors, but from female spectators who thought Annie's profession was not ladylike. "If they wished to be friendly they could," Annie later wrote of these women. "If they did not I did not care." When Annie picked up her gun at a competitive shoot, all she cared about was winning. And with rare exceptions, she always won.

Created in New York, this "cabinet card" of Annie featured her photo on the front and her biography on the back.

Despite her incredibly busy schedule, Annie sometimes took time out for fun. One cold winter day she decided to hitch up a sled to one of the Wild West's animals—a moose named Jerry—and go for a ride on the city streets. Jerry, however, was fond of apples. When he spotted pile of apples on a fruit seller's cart, the moose crashed into it. Annie had to pay the fruit seller five dollars for the loss of his produce. Given that she hated to part with a cent, it's safe to say she wasn't happy with Jerry.

Having conquered New York, Buffalo Bill set his sights on Europe. He booked the show for a European tour, with London, England, as the first stop. As the Wild West prepared to leave, Frank took out an advertisement in a New York newspaper. "Don't forget this," it proclaimed. "There is only one ANNIE OAKLEY. And she leaves for Europe with the Wild West."

chapter **8**

The Rifle Queen Conquers Europe

On March 31, 1887, Buffalo Bill's Wild West—including 160 horses and 16 buffalo—boarded the steamship *State of Nebraska* and set out across the Atlantic Ocean for London. For most of the performers, Annie included, this would be their first trip outside North America. Few of the 97 Indian members of the troupe had even seen the ocean. After a stormy crossing, the show set up its tents in the London district of Earl's Court.

The Wild West troupe poses on deck before sailing for Britain. Annie and Frank can be seen in the third row, at right.

The Wild West was part of the "American Exhibition," which in turn was part of a big fair celebrating the 50th anniversary of Queen Victoria's reign over Great Britain. Before the Wild West arrived, the American Exhibition had been pretty much a failure with the British public. It didn't offer anything more exciting than exhibits showcasing the products of American factories, like typewriters and clocks.

Queen Victoria

Queen Victoria reigned from 1837 to 1901, longer than any other British monarch. The Victorian Era, as this period is called, was a complex time, known for industrial advancements, the expansion of the British Empire, and strict standards of morality. Sadly, Victoria spent much of her reign in mourning for her husband, Prince Albert, who died in 1861.

The arrival of Buffalo Bill's show changed all that. Londoners and people from all over Britain flocked to Earl's Court to experience a bit of America's Wild West— or at least Buffalo Bill's version of it. In just six months, an astonishing 2.5 million people saw the show, and hundreds of thousands more attended when the Wild West made road trips to the cities of Manchester and Birmingham.

As with their American counterparts, Annie quickly won over British audiences. She was not the only featured shooter in the show—Lillian Smith, Johnny Baker, and Buffalo Bill

Prince Edward and Princess Alexandra became king and queen of Great Britain after Queen Victoria's death in 1901.

himself all had shooting acts. Still, in the words of a British reviewer, "The loudest applause of the night is reserved for Miss Annie Oakley, because her shooting entertainment is clever, precise and dramatic."

Soon, the girl hunter of Darke County found herself meeting some of the most famous people in the world. Edward, Prince of Wales (the heir to the British throne) and his wife Princess Alexandra attended a performance. According to tradition, anyone meeting the royal couple was supposed to greet the Prince first. When Annie was introduced to Edward and Alexandra, however, she made a point of shaking hands with the Princess first. "You'll have to excuse me, please," Annie told the Prince, "because I am an American and in America, ladies come first."

Some English newspapers sniffed that Annie had "insulted" the Prince. Others praised her action as an example of democratic American manners. But there was more to the story. It was widely known that the Prince was unfaithful to his wife. Annie didn't approve of that kind of behavior. Her break with tradition was a way of showing support for the Princess.

In any event, the episode didn't hurt the show's popularity. Later, Queen Victoria herself made a rare

CZAR

Derived from the Latin *Caesar*, *czar* was the title given to the ruler of Russia until the monarchy was overthrown in 1917.

public appearance to see a performance and met Annie. The queen declared her "a very clever little girl."

Annie also found herself pitted against another royal visitor to the American Exhibition: Grand Duke Michael, the son of Russia's czar, and a very good shot. While Cody and Nate Salsbury were nervous about Annie competing against a member of a royal family, Annie accepted the Duke's challenge to a 50-bird trap-shooting match. Annie brought down 47 birds; the Duke, 36.

Hunting and shooting were popular pastimes of Britain's upper classes, and between shows Annie was invited to take part in shoots at the country's elite sporting clubs. (Often, she was the first woman to set foot on their shooting ranges.) A couple of

This oil painting by Samuel Henry Aiken depicts a pigeon shoot in the English countryside.

times she lost matches because she wasn't used to shooting in the damp English weather, which could throw off the path of her shots. When she ordered several custom-made, lightweight shotguns from a master English gunmaker, Charles Lancaster, she became practically unbeatable. Annie also gave private shooting lessons to British women during this time.

When she didn't have a gun in her hand, Annie mingled with all classes of British society. Invited to fancy-dress balls and dinners, she insisted on wearing her own homemade dresses instead of gowns, and she charmed everyone with her modest manners. When she took walks on London's streets or rode her horse in the city's parks, she was amazed to hear people point her out and shout, "There goes the boss shooter!"

Annie's British admirers also showered her with presents. One gift was a St. Bernard puppy that Annie named Sir Ralph. The new dog helped ease the sadness of George the poodle's death.

Annie especially liked to host tea parties for the children of her

This photo shows Annie on horseback during the Wild West's first tour of Britain—riding sidesaddle.

new British friends. Annie's love for children and her kindness toward them would become a big part of her legend. She and Frank, however, never had children of their own. No one knows why. It may be that Frank or Annie simply couldn't have children because one or the other had some physical condition that remains unknown to this day. But the couple may have been childless by choice. They

lived a hectic life of constant travel. Perhaps they felt that if they did have children, they wouldn't be able to give them a secure, stable home in which to grow up.

There's no doubt, though, that Annie had a soft spot in her heart for kids. For example, when Johnny Baker's wife, Della, died, Annie took a close interest in the raising of his two daughters. She was also a fond and generous aunt to her sisters' children.

The Wild West's London run was one of the greatest triumphs in show-business history, and it spread Annie's fame to Europe and beyond. She liked England, too, telling an interviewer that "I know this much: that if I had my mother living with me here I should be in no hurry to get back to the States."

The show's success in London was really the turning point in Annie's career as a professional shooter. Even so, she wasn't entirely happy with life in the Wild West troupe. She still resented the fact that Lillian Smith was with the show (though she did have the satisfaction of outshooting her younger rival in a match held by Britain's Rifle Association at Wimbledon Common). Also, according to some accounts, she and Frank may have argued with Cody about money. And it's possible that Cody might have been jealous of Annie's success. He was proud of his own shooting skills, but, as a London newspaper put it, "[Annie's] marksmanship is better than Buffalo Bill's and her shooting is phenomenal." In later years, Annie would simply say that the story of her break with the Wild West was "too long to tell."

Whatever the reasons for their falling-out with Cody, Frank and Annie decided to leave Buffalo Bill's Wild West. They played their last show in London on Halloween 1887. "[Annie's] loss to the Wild West show will be a serious one," reported the *London Evening News*.

This was especially true because Annie was about to become even more famous than ever—although not in a way she liked. As Annie prepared to leave London, a British publisher brought out a short "biography" of her titled *The Rifle Queen*. There was hardly a true word in the book,

This photo of the Wild West—taken in London in 1887—gives an idea of the amazing variety of people who made up the troupe. Annie is circled near the front.

The scenes on the cover of *The Rifle Queen* give a clue as to its fabricated and inaccurate content.

which breathlessly described how Annie had faced down bandits and train robbers, and hunted panthers and wolves on the western plains. *The Rifle Queen* quickly became a best-seller.

Frank and Annie arrived in New York in December 1887. Annie spent a lot of the next year taking part in shooting competitions: She beat a champion British marksman, William Graham, in a best-of-three series. She also performed onstage at Tony Pastor's theater on New York's Fourteenth Street, and in vaudeville theaters in cities such as Boston and Philadelphia.

The success of Buffalo Bill's show in America led to the formation of several competing Wild West–themed shows. In June of 1888, Annie joined up with one such troupe— "Pawnee Bill's Historical Wild West Exhibition and Indian Encampment." Frank set up the deal in a hurry. There was less than a week for Annie to prepare before her first performance with the show, in New Jersey, on July 2, 1888. But that was time enough to print up posters proclaiming: "There is but one Annie Oakley—and she is with us . . . fresh from her London triumph with Buffalo Bill."

Although the Pawnee Bill show was probably the biggest and best of Cody's competitors, sometimes drawing as many as 12,000 people to a performance, it still wasn't in the same league as Buffalo Bill's Wild West, which had returned to America and was preparing for a tour of Europe in 1889.

Soon, Frank was talking to Cody and Nate Salsbury about the possibility of Annie returning to the Wild West. Cody was certainly eager to have her back; Annie's success with Pawnee Bill had proved her great popularity with audiences. In the end, Annie agreed to rejoin the Wild West. The fact that Lillian Smith had left the show probably helped seal the deal. The Pawnee Bill show struggled on a little longer without Annie, but by the end of the season it was bankrupt.

In February 1889 the Wild West headed back across the Atlantic. The first stop was France, for a run at the Paris Universal Exhibition—a world's fair celebrating the hundredth anniversary of the French Revolution. At first, it seemed like French audiences would be harder to please than English

Although they were show-business rivals, Buffalo Bill (right) and Pawnee Bill also maintained a friendship.

ones. When the Wild West began its first performance, the crowd of 20,000 people seemed bored— "they sat like icebergs at first," Annie later recalled. That changed when she began her shooting act. "As the first crack of the gun sent the stiff, flying targets to pieces," Annie wrote, "there came the 'ahs,' then the shots came so fast that cries of 'bravo!' went up."

Annie always took pride in keeping her tent ready for visitors, as shown in this photo taken in Paris in 1889.

The people of Paris soon took Annie to their hearts the way the people of London had. And once again, Annie met (and charmed) the high and mighty. The president of France told Annie that he'd make her an officer in the French Army if she ever decided to leave show business. The king of Senegal, one of France's colonies in Africa, wanted Annie to come home with him to shoot the tigers that sometimes killed his people.

After Paris, the Wild West toured around Europe for three years, visiting such countries as Germany, Italy, and Spain. The girl hunter from Ohio had come a long way. She rode gondolas in Venice and attended the opera in Vienna. Kings and queens, emperors and aristocrats, came to the shows and lined up to meet her afterward.

However, as she traveled, Annie became troubled by what she saw of European poverty. Just as Sitting Bull had been horrified to see the gap between the rich and poor in American cities, Annie was horrified to see that in some of the places the Wild West went, people were actually starving. In Spain, she witnessed women literally fighting over the garbage from the show's kitchen tent so they could feed their families. Annie quietly slipped them baskets of food. It was in Europe that Annie began her habit of giving money to orphanages and children's charities.

Annie was meeting people who lived in palaces, but life on the road with the Wild West was still far from luxurious. Frank and Annie spent most of their time on the train or in their tent. In Barcelona, Spain, Annie and many of her fellow performers got sick with the flu, and one—Frank Richmond, a good friend of Annie and Frank—died.

Buffalo Bill and some of the troupe's Indians tour the famous canals of Venice, Italy, in a gondola.

The Wild West's performers suffered from homesickness, too, during the long European tour. When the troupe was stuck in Barcelona, ravaged by the flu, Frank and Johnny Baker decided to put together a traditional American Christmas dinner. They managed to find a turkey, but even a whole bird didn't go far when divided up among so many people. "What was left of that turkey," Annie wrote, "wouldn't have served a gnat for dessert."

Kaiser Wilhelm

During the Wild West's European tour, Germany's Crown Prince Wilhelm asked Annie to shoot the ash off a cigarette in his mouth (or possibly in his hand), which she reluctantly did. She supposedly later said, "I didn't like that man—he looks like he could start a war." Sure enough, in 1914, when Wilhelm was kaiser (emperor) of Germany, he helped plunge Europe into World War I. As is so often the case with Annie, however, the story of her prophetic comment is probably too good to be true.

On the professional side, Annie got fed up with the poor quality of most European gunpowder, which threw off her shots and sometimes caused dangerous misfires. She preferred a high-quality grade of English gunpowder, but this was difficult to find: Most European countries prohibited imports of gunpowder in order to protect their own arms industries from competition. Annie got around this problem by having English friends send her packages of eggs—which came packed in her favorite powder.

When the Wild West wasn't performing, Annie and Frank took vacations in England. It was during one such break, in early 1891, when the mail brought an Ohio newspaper. Annie was shocked to see a headline that read, "Poor Anne Oakley dies in a far-off land—the greatest of the female shots."

In fact, an American singer named Anne Oatley had died in South America. A reporter with a French newspaper confused the two women, and then newspapers all over Europe and America reprinted the story. Annie was especially worried about the effect the story would have on her elderly mother.

Always a fan of everything British, Annie poses in an outfit of Scottish plaid during a trip to England's northern neighbor.

In those days, long before long-distance telephone calling and the Internet, the fastest way to communicate across oceans was by telegraph. Frank immediately sent word that the story was untrue. Still, it took days before newspapers in America corrected the story and Annie's grieving mother knew that her daughter was alive and well.

Annie would later laugh about the episode. But it was a reminder that fame carried a price.

chapter 9

Settling Down

The Wild West finished up its long European tour with another run in London. By now, the show was even bigger. Its new name was "Buffalo Bill's Wild West and Congress of Rough Riders of the World," and besides the usual cowboys and Indians, it included gauchos (South American cowboys), cossacks (mounted warriors from Russia), and even a detachment of cavalrymen from the U.S. Army.

But 31-year-old Annie was still the star, both for her skills and for her personality. And she always seemed to have a special connection with British audiences. "Miss Annie Oakley,"

The Wild West grew to include horsemen from around the world—including African warriors from Sudan.

wrote a British writer in the summer of 1892, "possesses one of the kindest and gentlest dispositions that one could ever wish to own. Her pleasant manner and her soft cheery voice are only excelled by her accuracy of aim . . . with the rifle."

Frank and Annie's house in Nutley. A pigeon that Annie had shot in England was mounted over the fireplace.

Annie, Frank, and the rest of the show arrived back in New York in October 1892. This time, Annie decided to stay with the Wild West. Because the show only toured America from late spring through fall, however, she and Frank would have plenty of time for their own projects. And after so many years of traveling constantly and living out of trunks and suitcases, they could finally put down some roots.

The couple bought some land in the town of Nutley, New Jersey, just a few miles from New York City, on the other side of the Hudson River. The community was popular with writers, artists, and show-business people because it offered country living while being close to the city. Annie herself helped design the house at 304 Grant Avenue, and she and Frank moved into it in December 1893, after the Wild West ended a hugely successful run at that year's World's Fair in Chicago.

ANNIE OAKLEY
RIDES THE

STERLING BICYCLE
"BUILT LIKE A WATCH"

An enthusiastic cyclist, Annie lent her name to an advertising campaign for Chicago's Sterling Cycle Works.

Annie and Frank quickly made friends with many of the residents of their new hometown. In March 1894, before the next Wild West tour began, Annie attracted thousands of spectators to Nutley when she agreed to perform in an amateur circus to raise money for charity.

Annie also pursued a new hobby: bicycling. (The modern "safety bicycle" had been invented just a few years before, starting a craze for "wheeling" in Europe and America.) Annie figured out how to shoot while cycling, and soon she was hitting targets from a bicycle seat as easily as she did from the saddle of a horse.

Bicycling also helped Annie, now in her mid-30s, stay in shape. She always took physical fitness seriously, and often recommended that women "go in for sport," as long as it didn't lead them to "neglect their homes." She also wrote, in 1897, "[I] think sport and healthful exercise make women better, healthier, and happier." Besides bicycling and walking, Annie swam and worked out with light weights. When she was on the road with the Wild West, Annie substituted her shotguns for weights in her exercise routine.

Annie didn't have to travel during the Wild West's 1894 season; the show set up in nearby Brooklyn. It also offered nighttime performances, under the electric lighting provided by one of Annie's New Jersey neighbors—the great inventor Thomas Edison.

Having perfected the lightbulb and the phonograph, Edison was now working on yet another world-changing invention—the kinetoscope, an early version of the movie camera. To test his invention, Edison invited performers to appear before the camera at his studio in West Orange, New Jersey. The performers included dancers, weightlifters, and even a vaudeville act called "Professor Welton and his Boxing Cats." In the fall of 1894, Edison filmed Annie shooting target balls.

For the next seven years, from 1894 to 1901, Annie and Frank's life followed a routine. From late March through October, they usually rented out the Nutley house and went on the road with the Wild West. Now the most popular traveling show in the world, the Wild West moved around the country in no less than three trains totaling 52 cars. In a typical year it stopped in 130 or so towns and cities. Life on

Annie blasts away in her historic performance in front of Thomas Edison's kinetoscope camera.

Thomas Edison

Inventing or improving such devices as the phonograph, the telephone, the movie camera, and the electric lightbulb, Thomas Edison (1847–1931) helped shaped the modern world. He also set up the world's first modern research laboratory in Menlo Park, New Jersey. The lab later moved to West Orange, which is where Annie performed for his camera.

the road was now more comfortable than in the old days: Annie and Frank had their own room in one of the train cars, complete with running water. But it was still a grueling schedule. The Wild West usually performed twice a day, and rarely stayed more than a few days in any one place. Annie was getting older and the pace was getting to her. But, as she told a reporter in 1899, "I have thought several times that I would not go with the show another year, but I always do."

In the off-season, Annie kept up a busy schedule of competitions and shooting lessons. She and Frank often took vacations in southern states like Arkansas, Virginia, and Tennessee, where Annie enjoyed hunting. She also spent time with her family in Ohio, both on vacation and when the Wild West toured the state.

In July 1900, Annie appeared in Greenville with the show. Her mother and sisters and many old Darke County friends and neighbors were in the audience. Afterward, the townspeople presented Annie with a silver trophy. She was so full of emotion she could barely speak. That night, she told a local reporter, "I have received and won many medals from many sources, all of which I prize very highly, but this cup takes the foreground. I prize it more highly than anything ever presented to me."

In October 1901, Annie and Frank were asleep in their room on one of the Wild West trains as it chugged through the Virginia countryside. Suddenly there was a tremendous crash, throwing them to the floor.

The Wild West train had smashed head-on into a train coming down the same track in the opposite direction. Amazingly, none of the show's people were killed. The animals were not so lucky; about 100 horses in the head cars of the train were killed in the accident.

Just what happened to Annie in this incident is yet another of her life's mysteries. Early

Train wrecks like the one the Wild West suffered in 1901 were an all-too-common occurrence in America at the time.

accounts of the crash said that "all members of the Wild West show escaped injury," and that Annie had only been shaken up. But there were other reports that she'd suffered a serious injury to her hip or back and had to have surgery. If Annie was hurt, she recovered quickly: Two months later she took part in a match in New Jersey. A legend also sprang up that the shock of the accident made Annie's brown hair turn white within hours.

Although not shy about displaying her medals and awards, Annie claimed the cup given to her at Greenville meant the most to her.

This is almost certainly not true, because the first report of the change in her hair color didn't appear in newspapers until more than a year later. Another story is that her hair changed color when she accidentally stayed too long in a "scalding" bath at a spa in Arkansas—and she was too embarrassed to admit it. But, however it happened, her hair did turn totally white around this time. For years afterward, Annie wore a brown wig.

Whatever really happened during the train crash and afterward, Annie took it as a sign that the time had come call it quits with what she called "the dear old Wild West."

After her departure, Annie kept in touch with some members of the Wild West troupe, such as Cody and Johnny Baker. In April 1902, however, she ran into someone she was probably not hoping to see: Lillian Smith, her old rival. The years had not been kind to Lillian. By this time she was performing in a show called "Mexican Joe's Wild West," billed as "Princess Wenona, the Indian Girl Shot"—even though she was now in her thirties and not an American Indian. Along with about 500 others, Annie and Lillian both took part in one of the country's major shooting competitions, the Grand American Handicap, a trap-shooting event that took place in Kansas City, Missouri. As she had done in London 15 years earlier, Annie outshot Lillian. The two never met again.

This hand-colored photograph shows that, even near the end of his career, Buffalo Bill lost none of his famous charisma.

Meanwhile, the Wild West continued on until 1913, when money troubles finally forced its closing. Buffalo Bill Cody died four years later. "Goodbye old friend," Annie wrote, "The sun setting over the mountains will pay its tribute to the resting place of the last of the great builders of the West, all of which you loved, and part of which you were."

10

"Some One Will Pay for this Dreadful Mistake"

After leaving the Wild West show, Annie started on a new career—as an actress. In fact, she was no stranger to acting. When she and Frank had performed together as Butler & Oakley, they often did short comedy skits in addition to their shooting act. In 1888, in Philadelphia, Annie had acted in a western-themed play titled *Deadwood Dick, or the Sunbeam of the Sierras,* in which she played a white child raised by Indians. And in 1895, she appeared on stage in London in *Miss Rora,* a play that was really just a showcase for her shooting.

Now, in 1902, she had a play written just for her—*The Western Girl.* Set in the Rocky Mountains, *The Western Girl* was one of the "melodramas" popular in America at

the time, filled with thrilling action and sentimental scenes. In it, Annie played herself—or

A poster for *The Western Girl* shows Annie throwing a lasso over the female villain at the edge of a cliff.

rather the legendary
version of herself.
Her character, Nance
Garner, struggled
against her outlaw
father and battled
various bandits while
falling in love with
a handsome cavalry
soldier. The play
opened in Elizabeth,
New Jersey,
in November.

Annie (in a brown wig) gets
another villain in her sights
in this scene from *The
Western Girl*.

Like *Miss Rora*,
The Western Girl gave Annie the
chance to show off her shooting and
horseback riding skills—although during one performance,
she lost control of her horse and got a deep cut on her nose
when the animal crashed into a piece of scenery. With her
typical determination, Annie finished the show after some
first aid from a doctor in the audience.

Life seemed good to Annie and Frank in the summer of
1903. While *The Western Girl* didn't run for very long and
never made it to Broadway, audiences loved it, and most of
the reviews were good. Frank was happy in his new job as a
kind of salesman for the Union Metallic Cartridge Company
(UMC), a firm that made ammunition.

And then, on August 11, 1903, Annie once again picked up a newspaper and read a headline that shocked her: "Annie Oakley asks court for mercy . . . steals to secure cocaine." The story had it that Annie was in jail in Chicago, charged with stealing a pair of pants which she hoped to sell for money to buy drugs. Before long the story spread to newspapers all over the county.

Still dashingly handsome in late middle age, Frank Butler enjoyed his job working for the UMC company.

Annie was beyond horrified. When the false reports of her death hit newspapers in 1890, she had worried mainly about the effect on her friends and family. But in this case, her reputation was at stake. And Annie took her reputation very seriously. She wasn't just proud of her fame—she was proud of the way she'd achieved that fame. All her life she'd stuck to the Quaker values she'd learned from her parents in Darke County—like refusing to wear revealing costumes in her act. She believed in leading a wholesome, upright life, and she wanted to be an example to others. And now, millions of people were hearing that she was a thief and a drug addict. "That terrible piece . . .

FRAUD

A fraud is an act of deceit or trickery involving a distortion of the truth, or someone who perpetrates such an act.

nearly killed me," she once said. "The only thing that kept me alive was the desire to [clear] my character."

Like the 1890 reports of her death, the story was a case of mistaken identity. The woman in jail was a small-time actress who sometimes performed under the name "Any Oakley."

Annie had barely finished reading the story before she began firing off letters to the newspapers that had printed it. The very next day, she wrote the editor of a Brooklyn paper: "Woman posing as Annie Oakley is a fraud . . . and I have not been to Chicago since last winter. . . . Now that you have done me an injustice in publishing that article, I hope you will contradict it."

Some newspapers did correct the story right away. Others never believed it in the first place. Her hometown newspaper in Greenville, Ohio, simply said the report was "too absurd for belief." But many other papers didn't bother to make the truth known. This made Annie furious. As she wrote to a Philadelphia paper, "Some one will pay for this dreadful mistake."

Annie went after these newspapers with even more determination than she'd shown stalking quail back in Darke

This newspaper article, and others like it, launched Annie's long, costly legal battle to uphold her reputation.

ANNIE OAKLEY'S DOWNFALL.

Annie Oakley, daughter-in-law of "Buffalo Bill" and the most famous woman rifle shot in the world, is locked up in a cell at the Harrison street station in Chicago under a Bridewell sentence for stealing the trousers of a negro in order to get money with which to buy cocaine.

Annie Oakley was seen in Belleville on the occasion of Buffalo Bill's visit to this city, several years ago, and proved a great attraction by her remarkable shooting.

When arrested she gave the name of Elizabeth Cody, but it occurred to no one to connect her with Col.Cody's famous daughter-in-law. However, when brought before Justice Caverly, she admitted her guilt and begged the court to have pity on her. The once striking beauty of the woman is now entirely gone. Although she is but 25 years old, she looks almost 40. Hers, in fact, is one of the most extreme cases which have come up in Chicago police circles.

County. She sued every paper—55 in all—that didn't take back the story.

This legal battle took up much of the next seven years of Annie's life as she traveled around the country testifying in court. In the end, she won all but one case—although some cases were settled out of court. While Annie won a lot of money in settlements and damages, she probably spent at least the same amount on lawyers and other expenses. As important as money was to Annie, she put a higher value on her reputation. And finally, by 1910, she'd cleared her name to her satisfaction.

"There were months when I prayed to God every day to only spare my reason so as to let me clear myself of this," she said at the height of her legal troubles, "and I will do this."

Whenever she could find the time, she continued her shooting career. In 1906, she joined Frank on the UMC's shooting team, which traveled around the country to win publicity for the company's products. In an exhibition that year, she shot 1,016 brass disks in a row.

Annie and Frank sold the house in Nutley in 1904. Keeping up the house seemed a waste of money; between their shooting careers and the ongoing lawsuits, neither of them was at home much anyway. And as Annie herself said, she "went to pieces over the care of a household."

During the years with the Wild West, visitors to the show's encampment often marveled at the tent Annie and Frank shared: It was always neat, clean, and well furnished. But a tent is a tent and a house is a house. It seems that Annie got fed up with the daily routine of running a house—especially managing servants. (At the time, most Americans who could afford to do so employed cooks, housekeepers, and other "help.") So for the next few years Annie and Frank lived in rented houses and apartments.

Annie turned 50 years of age in 1910. America was a very different place than it had been when she was growing up in Darke County. When she was born in 1860, the nation's population was 31.4 million people. In 1910 it stood at more than 92 million. Just a couple of decades earlier, inventions like electric lighting and the telephone were mostly luxuries for the rich. Now they could be found in many American homes. Automobiles—such as Henry Ford's Model T, which first appeared in 1908—were rapidly replacing horses on America's streets and roads. The dream of flight was now a reality, too, thanks to Orville and Wilbur Wright.

Despite all these changes, Americans still loved to be entertained by tales of the Wild West—an era that was now truly in the past. Audiences now had a new way to get that entertainment—the movies. Thomas

In 1908, Annie sent this custom-made postcard from Amityville, Long Island, where she and Frank had a friend.

Here, Annie gives Dorothy Stone—daughter of her friend Fred Stone—a shooting lesson on Long Island.

John Philip Sousa, between sessions of golfing, hunting, and horseback riding. Annie also gave shooting lessons to the hotel's female guests most mornings.

As always, Annie believed strongly that it was important for women to learn how to use guns—not only as a form of healthy mental and physical exercise, but to be able to defend themselves from attackers. Later, Annie would say that she figured she'd taught more than 15,000 women to shoot over the course of her life.

In many ways Annie was a very modern woman. She'd made her own way in the world since she was a young girl. She was proud of her success and proud of the example she'd set for other women. She also believed that men and women should be equal in the workplace. As she once said, "I have always maintained that outside of heavy . . . labor, anything a man can do a woman can do practically as well."

In other ways, though, Annie held old-fashioned attitudes. This is especially true of her views about the growing movement to win the right to vote for all American women.

Suffrage is the right to vote. A supporter of women's suffrage believes that women should be given this right.

By now, women's suffrage was a big political issue. While some states did allow women to vote, the right to vote still wasn't guaranteed nationwide. American "suffragists" like Alice Paul, leader of the National Women's Party, did things like chain themselves to the fence around the White House to win attention for their cause. Demonstrations like these often led to the suffragists being thrown in jail—and being force-fed when they went on hunger strikes.

Annie was one of the most famous women in America, so naturally the women's rights movement hoped for her public support. The press was also interested in what she had to say—but Annie always tried to avoid the subject. "About [women's suffrage] she does not have much to say," one reporter wrote. "But you get the impression that she has never been strong for equal rights as this generation understands the term." When pressed, Annie might say that women's suffrage would only be a

Women's suffrage supporters (including Alice Paul, top) celebrate the ratification of the 19th Amendment.

The Red Cross

In 1863, Swiss businessman Henri Dunant established an international organization, the Red Cross, to provide aid for those suffering from the ravages of war. Five years later, Clara Barton—a nurse in the Civil War—set up the U.S. branch. During World War I, the American Red Cross provided more than 24,000 nurses for service with the U.S. forces, supplied aid to prisoners of war, and established recreational centers in military camps both at home and overseas.

good thing "if only the good women voted." (Eventually, the 19th Amendment to the U.S. Constitution, which became law in 1920, won the vote for all American women.)

In 1914, World War I broke out in Europe. For almost three years, the United States stayed out of the fight. After German submarines began sinking American ships, however, Congress declared war on Germany in April 1917.

After war was declared, Annie contacted the War Department in Washington, offering to organize a unit of woman sharpshooters for "home defense." The government never bothered to reply. But Annie was determined to do as much as she could for the war effort. She even volunteered to tour army training camps and demonstrate shooting techniques—and this time, the government agreed.

All of the young soldiers knew her by reputation. Some might have seen her shoot during her years with the Young

Buffalo Wild West show. But they were still amazed to see this tiny, white-haired woman in her late 50s (Annie had put aside her brown wig) step up to the firing line and effortlessly hit her targets, whether she was using a rifle, a shotgun, or a pistol.

Annie rejoiced in her new role. "I'm the happiest woman in the world," she said, "because I had the opportunity to 'do my bit' in a way which was best suited to me."

Dave the English setter "did his bit," too, by raising money for the Red Cross. When Annie gave performances, people in the audience were invited to wrap coins or bills in a handkerchief and present the handkerchief to Dave to smell. Then the audience would hide the handkerchiefs around the area, and Dave would sniff them out, with the money going to the Red Cross. Dave's ability was amazing. On one occasion, he found more than $1,600. "He never fails," wrote one reporter. The setter quickly became famous in his own right as "Dave, the Red Cross dog."

This Red Cross poster from World War I praises Dave the dog for his fund-raising efforts and encourages others to do their part.

chapter 12

The Final Years

Annie and Frank were at Pinehurst when the war ended on November 11, 1918. The hotel guests and local residents celebrated with a parade, and Annie gave a shooting exhibition.

With the war over, Annie gave more of her time to charity. Now, when she did appear on shooting ranges, it was to raise money for causes that were close to her heart—like the fight against tuberculosis, the lung disease that had killed two of her sisters. She even melted down the gold medals she'd won in competitions, donating the money to a hospital for tuberculosis patients in Montrose, North Carolina, not far from Pinehurst. She also visited the patients and brought them gifts.

Annie never liked to draw attention to her good works,

Annie and Frank display the results from a hunt at Pinehurst, North Carolina, in this photo from around 1920.

Frank tosses up targets and Annie shoots them down at a shooting demonstration at the Pinehurst gun club.

although the media often found out about them. A few years earlier, for example, a Massachusetts newspaper reported that Annie had "adopted" 18 children. The newspaper didn't have its facts straight. The truth was that Annie was quietly paying for the education of 18 or 19 young women. Annie's regrets about her own lack of a formal education probably led her to these acts of generosity.

And Annie didn't forget the young men she'd performed for as they trained to go overseas and into combat in World War I. On July 1, 1922, she took part in a big show on Long Island, New York, to raise money to help care for the soldiers who'd come home from the war lacking limbs, sight, or hearing. A reporter for the *New York Tribune* newspaper, recalling Annie's stints with Wild West shows, wrote of how the young woman of years past was now a "white-haired, sweet-voiced little woman in a black dress." But she still blasted the targets that Frank threw in the air with the greatest of ease. This didn't surprise anyone in the world of competitive shooting. A few months before, on a Maryland trap-shooting range,

Annie had downed 100 clay pigeons in a row—a women's world record at the time.

In fact, Annie—now 62 years old—was probably considering yet another show-business comeback. She was still talking about performing in the movies. And in October 1922, she performed in front of about 100,000 people in a fair in Brockton, Massachusetts. Except for shows put on to raise money for the war effort or charity, it was her first public exhibition in years.

Whatever plans Annie had were cut short on the night of November 9, 1922. Driving north from Leesburg, Florida, the car in which Annie and Frank were riding got forced off the road and flipped over. Her right hip and ankle were broken. She spent the next two months in a hospital in Daytona, Florida, with Frank and Dave (who weren't injured in the crash) by her side.

From all over the country, people rushed to wish her well. "Since my accident, I have received nearly 2,000 letters and telegrams, also loads of flowers from many kind and thoughtful friends," Annie wrote. "Only someone like myself, who has suffered and laid

Annie sent a friend this postcard from Florida while recovering from her injuries.

for weeks in a hospital, knows what such messages of sympathy mean and I certainly do appreciate all that my friends have done for me."

By February 1923 Annie was able to get around on crutches. But her injuries were permanent. From now on, she had to wear a metal brace on her right leg.

Annie, Frank, and Dave went back to Leesburg. One day, while walking with Frank, Dave—ever the hunter—chased a squirrel into the street. A car hit and killed him. Annie and Frank grieved at the loss of their companion—and performing partner—of 10 years.

In this photo, an aging Annie wears a necklace given to her by King Ludwig II of the German state of Bavaria.

Not long after she got out of the hospital, Annie recovered enough to take part in occasional shoots—including a performance for the Philadelphia Phillies baseball team, who were in Leesburg for spring training. Over the next couple of years Annie and Frank still traveled, and they helped found the American Trapshooting Association.

"For me," Annie told an interviewer around this time, "sitting still is harder than any kind of work." But Annie was definitely slowing down. Now that she was more or less fully retired, she decided to return to Ohio. She and

In this photo from 1920, Annie, Frank, and the trusty Dave are shown as a happy and harmonious family.

Frank lived with one of Annie's nieces in Darke County before moving to a house in Dayton. She decided to write her autobiography, and Frank contacted a professional writer to help her with it, but she only managed to write a few pages.

By now Annie was suffering from anemia—a lack of red blood cells. The disease left her "pale and weak." Her doctor ordered her to "remain absolutely quiet." Some of Annie's biographers also think that she was suffering from a form of lead poisoning as a result of decades of handling buckshot and bullets.

Although she was now too ill to join him, Annie insisted that Frank make a planned trip to North Carolina in the fall of 1926. Frank had health problems of his own, however, and he didn't get farther than Detroit, Michigan, where another of Annie's nieces cared for him. Meanwhile, Annie moved to Greenville.

Annie sensed the end was near, and with her usual clear-headedness and determination, she faced up to it. She made her own funeral arrangements (she decided she wanted to be cremated) and divided up the souvenirs of her long career among her friends and relatives.

On the night of November 3, 1926, Annie died in her sleep. She was 66 years old.

Frank died in Michigan just 18 days later. While it's true that his health had been failing for some time, some accounts say he simply stopped eating when he heard of Annie's death.

"After traveling through 14 countries and appearing before all the royalty and nobility," Annie once said, "I have only one wish today. That is when my eyes are closed in death that they will bury me back in that quiet little farm land where I was born."

Annie got her wish. Her ashes were buried along with Frank's body in a small cemetery in what was once the village of North Star, Ohio. Her tombstone bears only her name, the year of her death, and the words "At Rest."

Annie and Frank are united in death as they were in life. Two of Annie's brothers are buried between them.

ANNIE OAKLEY
1926
AT REST

FRANK E. BUTLER
1926
AT REST

MOSES

JOHN
1888 – 1893

CLETUS
1893 – 1894

chapter 13

Annie Oakley's Legacy

Annie Oakley died in 1926, but her legacy—and her legend—endures to this day.

Over the last 80 years, books, movies, Broadway musicals, TV shows, comic books, board games—even a book of cut-out paper dolls—have all celebrated Annie's amazing life and career. Annie had been dead for less than 10 years when the first movie based on her life, *Annie Oakley*, hit theaters in 1935, with actress Barbara Stanwyck playing Annie.

Annie Oakley's plot centered on the romance between and Annie and Frank Butler, who was called "Toby Walker" in the movie. While the movie was pure fiction, Hollywood-style, some people who had known Annie felt that Stanwyck did capture something of Annie's true personality.

After the United States entered World War II in 1941, many Americans remembered Annie's contributions to the nation's previous war effort. In this new conflict, millions of women went

This statue erected by the Annie Oakley Foundation in Greenville, Ohio, honors Darke County's most famous resident.

to work in factories and plants making war materials, taking the place of men fighting overseas. In addition, more than 350,000 women served in branches of the military. American women now proved what Annie had always believed—that they could do most jobs as well as men. The United States government even honored Annie's memory by naming a cargo ship after her. Launched in Los Angeles in August 1943, the *Annie Oakley* was sunk by a German submarine in the English Channel in April 1945.

Just after the war, Annie served as the inspiration for one of the most successful Broadway musicals of all time. With words and music by Irving Berlin, *Annie Get Your Gun* opened at the Imperial Theater in New York City on May 16, 1946, and ran for 1,147 performances—a record at the time. A huge hit thanks to show-stopping songs like "There's No Business Like Show Business" and "Anything You Can Do," *Annie Get Your Gun* established Annie's legend in the minds of a new generation.

As with the 1935 movie, though, the onstage Annie

This famous poster from World War II encouraged American women to contribute to the country's defense industries.

We Can Do It!

WAR PRODUCTION CO-ORDINATING COMMITTEE

With her brassy voice and flashy costumes, Ethel Merman had little in common with the real Annie Oakley.

was "loosely based" on the real person. When a former neighbor of Annie's from Nutley remarked that Annie's actual life would make an even "more fabulous" story than the Broadway version, actress Ethel Merman, who played Annie in the show, said that "if the show included all of Annie's hardships it would be a melodrama, and I'd be a wreck." The musical returned to Broadway in 1966 (still featuring Ethel Merman) and again in 1999, with Bernadette Peters in the title role. The 1999 production won a Tony Award for Best Revival of a Musical.

After its original Broadway run, MGM Studios released a movie version of *Annie Get Your Gun* in 1950, with Betty Hutton playing Annie and Howard Keel playing Frank. The movie was even more of a departure from reality than the stage version. For example, it showed Annie wearing makeup and, in one scene, a low-cut gown—things that would have shocked the real Annie.

In the 1950s, television arrived on the American scene in a big way, and TV shows set in the Wild West proved to be just as popular as movie Westerns. From 1954 to 1957, the CBS network presented a weekly series called *Annie Oakley and*

Tagg. This TV version of Annie's early life portrayed her as a high-spirited girl with blonde pigtails, growing up on a ranch in Texas with her brother. While boys were the big audience for TV westerns, the show was just as popular with girls, and its success led to a series of children's books and comics with Annie as the heroine.

By the 1970s, many Americans came to question the romantic view of the American Wild West as seen in the movies and on TV. Filmmakers and writers now tried to show the West as it really was, and to separate fact from fiction in telling the life stories of legendary western personalities—including Annie.

Also, in the 1960s and 1970s, many American women began calling for more equality between the sexes. Despite some of her more

Betty Hutton's portrayal of Annie dancing in American Indian costume was even further from reality.

traditional views, Annie seemed like an ideal example to many in this feminist movement. She'd overcome great hardships to win worldwide fame through sheer talent and determination, in a field that was considered to be "men's work."

All this led people to wonder: Who was the real Annie Oakley?

By now, many biographies of Annie had appeared. Some biographers tried to uncover the facts. Others just repeated the same old stories, many of which were untrue or exaggerated. The problem facing anyone who tries to discover the real Annie Oakley is that there are so many differing accounts of the events of her life. Annie herself often told conflicting stories in her writings and in interviews with reporters.

The person who has probably come closest to answering the question "Who was the real Annie Oakley?" is Kansas journalist Shirl Kasper. Her carefully researched 1992 biography of Annie corrected many of the myths about her life and career.

The Buffalo Bill Historical Center in Cody, Wyoming, preserves the legacy of Buffalo Bill and his most famous performer.

In 2005, Larry McMurtry—author of the classic Western novel *Lonesome Dove* and many other books—published *The Colonel and Little Missie.* In telling the stories of both Buffalo Bill and Annie, he made the point that the two were the "first American superstars." In his words, "Annie Oakley, in the days just before the movies took off, was as popular as any actress. . . . For most of her sixteen seasons with Buffalo Bill's Wild West, she was probably the most celebrated female performer in the world."

The most remarkable aspect of Annie's rise to superstardom was how she achieved it. Sometimes she did

Annie Oakley strikes a memorable pose, in a photo that was later used as the model for a poster.

have to give in to the demands of a show-business career, and she was certainly uncomfortable with some of the things that came along with fame. But for the most part, she remained true to herself and to the values she'd learned growing up in Ohio.

Annie herself said it best in her personal motto:

"Aim at a high mark and you'll hit it. No, not the second time and maybe not the third. But keep on aiming and keep on shooting for only practice will make you perfect. Finally, you'll hit the bull's eye of success."

Events in the Life of Annie Oakley

1881
Annie meets (and beats) Frank Butler in a shooting match near Greenville, Ohio.

August 13, 1860
Annie is born (as Phoebe Ann Moses) in Darke County, Ohio.

1866
Annie's father dies.

1870
Annie is sent to the Darke County Infirmary.

1889–1892
Annie returns to the Wild West and spends three years touring Europe.

Late 1890 to early 1891
Annie combats rumors that she'd died in South America.

1887
After a triumphant run in Britain, Annie temporarily leaves the Wild West show.

BUTLER & OAKLEY.

1882–84
Annie and Frank marry and tour together as Butler & Oakley.

1868
Annie teaches herself how to shoot.

1885
Annie joins Buffalo Bill's Wild West.

1892
Returning to the United States, Annie and Frank build a house in Nutley, New Jersey.

1911–1913
Annie performs with the Young Buffalo Wild West Show.

November 21, 1926
Frank Butler dies in Detroit, Michigan.

1902
Annie takes to the stage in the melodrama *The Western Girl*.

1917–1918
Annie helps the U.S. war effort in World War I by giving exhibitions at army training camps.

1901
After a train wreck, Annie quits the Wild West.

1903–1910
Annie defends her reputation in court following newspaper reports that she'd been arrested for theft.

November 29, 1922
Annie is injured when her car overturns on a Florida road.

1913
Annie and Frank buy a house in Cambridge, Maryland.

1894
Thomas Edison films Annie shooting in his New Jersey studio.

November 3, 1926
Annie dies of anemia in Greenville, Ohio.

Bibliography

Kasper, Shirl. *Annie Oakley*. Norman, Oklahoma: The University of Oklahoma Press, 1992.

McMurtry, Larry. *The Colonel and Little Missie*. New York: Simon & Schuster, 2005.

Macy, Sue. *Bull's-Eye: A Photobiography of Annie Oakley*. Washington, D.C.: National Geographic Society, 2001.

Ridley, Glenda. *The Life and Legacy of Annie Oakley*. Norman, Oklahoma: The University of Oklahoma Press, 1994.

Warren, Louis S. *Buffalo Bill's America*. New York: Alfred A. Knopf, 2005.

Works Cited

p.13: "God intended women to be outside . . ." Kasper, 154–155. p.14: "With the reins around his neck . . ." Macy, 10. p.14: "But every night . . ." Riley, 5. p.16: "Stuffed in enough [gun] powder . . ." Riley, 7. p.16: "I still consider it . . ." Kasper, 4. p.16: "My mother . . ." Kasper, 5. p.18: "I don't know how I acquired the skill . . ." Riley, 12. p.18: "Somehow we managed to struggle along . . ." Riley, 6. p.20: "Wolves in sheep's clothing . . ." Riley, 7. p.21: "I got up at 4 o'clock . . ." Kasper, 6. p.21: "[I] got down on my little knees . . ." Macy, 16. p.22: "I was held a prisoner . . ." Riley, 7. p.22: "One fine spring day . . ." Riley, 7. p.23: "I prayed to God . . ." Riley, 8. p.24: "happy . . ." Riley, 9. p.25: "By a kerosene light . . ." Riley, 10. p.26: "I was homesick . . ." Riley, 11. p.27: "For the rest of her life . . ." McMurtry, 147. p.28: "Oh, how grand God's beautiful earth . . ." Riley, 11. p.30: "You must have your mind . . ." Kasper, 30. p.31: "Every mail day . . ." Macy, 17. p.36: "You may bet . . ." Kasper, 16. p.37: "Right then and there . . ." Macy, 19. . p.38: "There's a charming little girl . . ." Kasper, 17. p.40: "I went on with Mr. B. . . ." Riley, 21. p.40: "I didn't teach her how to shoot . . ." Kasper, 23–24. p.48: "The premier shots . . ." Kasper, 27. p.55–56: "Cody became a symbol . . ." Kasper, 35–36. p.59: "[All] shooting acts walked a line . . ." Warren, 240. p.60: "'Fine! Wonderful!' . . ." Kasper, 38. p.60: "I afterwards heard . . ." Kasper, 39. p.61: "Every head bowed before me . . ." Kasper, 39–40. p.62: "[The] kindest hearted, broadest minded . . ." Kasper, 210. . p.65: "[The] last shot only missed . . ." Kasper, 42. p.65: "[Finger] touch on the trigger . . ." Kasper, 43. . p.66: "He is a dear, faithful old friend . . ." Kasper, 53. p.67: "[B]etter than staying home . . ." McMurtry, 177. . p.68: "[G]ood coffee, bread, butter . . ." Riley, 33. p.69: "Some thought that Annie . . ." McMurtry, 143. p.72: "It was up–hill work . . ." Kasper, 66. p.73: "If they wished to be friendly . . ." Kasper, 67. p.73: "There is only one ANNIE OAKLEY . . ." Kasper, 68. p.76: "The loudest applause of the night . . ." Macy, 33. p.76: "You'll have to excuse me, please . . ." Kasper, 76. p.77: "[A] very clever little girl . . . " Kasper, 80. p.78: "There goes the boss shooter" Kasper, 77. p.79: "[I]mpossible to shoot brilliantly . . ." Riley, 114. p.79–80: "I know this much . . ." Kasper, 80. p.80–81: "[Annie's

marksmanship is better than Buffalo Bill's . . ." Kasper, 87. p.81: "too long to tell" Kasper, 91.
p.81: "[Annie's] loss to the Wild West show . . ." Kasper, p, 92. p.82: "There is but one Annie
Oakley . . ." Riley, 44. p.84: "they sat like icebergs at first" Kasper, 104. p.84: "As the first crack
of the gun . . ." Riley, 46. p.86: "What was left of that turkey . . ." Kasper, 112. p.87: "Poor Anne
Oakley . . ." Kasper, 113. p.88: "Miss Annie Oakley . . ." Macy, 43. p.90: "[I] think sport and
healthful exercise . . ." Riley, 141. p.92: "I have thought several times . . ." Macy, 46. p.93: "I have
received and won . . ." Kasper, 159. p.95: "Goodbye old friend . . ." McMurtry, 229. p.97–98:
"Annie Oakley asks court for mercy . . ." Kasper, 173. p.98: "That terrible piece . . ." Kasper, 175.
p.99: "Woman posing as Annie Oakley . . ." Kasper, 175. p.99. "too absurd for belief" Kasper,
176. p.99: "Some one will pay . . ." Macy, 48. p.100: "There were months when I prayed to God
. . ." Kasper, 179. . p.103: "[It] remained for the veteran Annie Oakley . . ." Kasper, 192. p.103:
"She is bright and alert . . ." Kasper, 191. . p.104: "a member of the family" Riley, 177. p.104–
105: "We did enjoy the boating and fishing . . ." Kasper, 198. p.106: "I have always maintained .
. ." Kasper, 214. p.107: "About [women's suffrage] . . ." Kasper, 213. p.107–108: "if only the good
women voted" Kasper, 213. p.109: "I'm the happiest woman in the world . . ." Kasper, 216–217.
p.109: "He never fails . . ." Kasper, 218. p.111: "[A] white–haired, sweet–voiced little woman . . ."
Kasper, 225. p.112: "Since my accident . . ." Kasper, 229. p.114: "After traveling through fourteen
countries . . . " Kasper, 237. p.118: "If the show included all of Annie's hardships . . ."Riley, 216.
p.121: "Annie Oakley, in the days just before the movies . . ." McMurtry, 5. p.121: "Aim at a high
mark . . ." Kasper, 232

For Further Study

Annie was the subject of an episode in the Public Broadcasting System's *American Experience*
television series. The DVD is available for purchase. The accompanying Web site is at:
www.pbs.org/wgbh/amex/oakley/

Annie was also the subject of a 1998 episode of the A&E Network's *Biography* series ("Annie
Oakley: Crackshot In Petticoats"). It's also available on DVD.

Two mostly fictional versions of Annie's life—the 1950 movie version of the musical *Annie
Get Your Gun* and the 1950s TV series—are likewise now on DVD.

You can visit the Annie Oakley Foundation's website at www.annieoakleyfoundation.org.
Located in Greenville, Ohio, the foundation hopes to build a museum and activity center. The
foundation also produced a DVD about Annie's life.

Also located in Greenville, the Garst Museum (has a permanent exhibition devoted to Annie.
Their Web site is at: www.garstmuseum.org

The Buffalo Bill Historical Center in Cody, Wyoming, is home to many artifacts related to
Annie, including her original scrapbooks. For more information, visit: www.bbhc.org

Index

Author's Note

Although this book is based on the most up-to-date and carefully researched sources available, there's still a lot about Annie Oakley's life that we just don't know, and accounts of events in her life and career sometimes disagree. Throughout the book, I've done my best to present a full picture of a subject who was in many ways a very private woman, while at the same time making clear the often-frustrating limitations of our knowledge.

Acknowledgments

The author wishes to thank Beth Sutinis for thinking of me to write this book; Alisha Neuhaus for getting the project started; John Searcy for bringing it to completion, and also for his superb editorship; Dirk Kaufman for his awesome design skills, as well as his friendship; Mark Johnson Davies for his equally awesome design skills and superhuman speed; Dr. Juti Winchester at the Buffalo Bill Historic Center for her expert advice; and, as always, Rachel, for her support in every way.

Picture Credits

About the Author

Chuck Wills is a writer, editor, and consultant specializing in American history. His books include *Destination America,* a history of immigration to the United States (a companion volume to the PBS series), *The Illustrated History of Weaponry, America's Presidents,* and *Lincoln: The Presidential Archives.* He lives in New York City.

Other DK Biographies you'll enjoy:

Charles Darwin
David C. King
ISBN 978-0-7566-2554-2 paperback
ISBN 978-0-7566-2555-9 hardcover

Princess Diana
Joanne Mattern
ISBN 978-0-7566-1614-4 paperback
ISBN 978-0-7566-1613-7 hardcover

Amelia Earhart
Tanya Lee Stone
ISBN 978-0-7566-2552-8 paperback
ISBN 978-0-7566-2553-5 hardcover

Albert Einstein
Frieda Wishinsky
ISBN 978-0-7566-1247-4 paperback
ISBN 978-0-7566-1248-1 hardcover

Gandhi
Amy Pastan
ISBN 978-0-7566-2111-7 paperback
ISBN 978-0-7566-2112-4 hardcover

Harry Houdini
Vicki Cobb
ISBN 978-0-7566-1245-0 paperback
ISBN 978-0-7566-1246-7 hardcover

Helen Keller
Leslie Garrett
ISBN 978-0-7566-0339-7 paperback
ISBN 978-0-7566-0488-2 hardcover

John F. Kennedy
Howard S. Kaplan
ISBN 978-0-7566-0340-3 paperback
ISBN 978-0-7566-0489-9 hardcover

Martin Luther King, Jr.
Amy Pastan
ISBN 978-0-7566-0342-7 paperback
ISBN 978-0-7566-0491-2 hardcover

Abraham Lincoln
Tanya Lee Stone
ISBN 978-0-7566-0834-7 paperback
ISBN 978-0-7566-0833-0 hardcover

Nelson Mandela
Lenny Hort & Laaren Brown
ISBN 978-0-7566-2109-4 paperback
ISBN 978-0-7566-2110-0 hardcover

Pelé
James Buckley Jr.
ISBN 978-0-7566-2987-8 paperback
ISBN 978-0-7566-2996-0 hardcover

Eleanor Roosevelt
Kem Knapp Sawyer
ISBN 978-0-7566-1496-6 paperback
ISBN 978-0-7566-1495-9 hardcover

George Washington
Lenny Hort
ISBN 978-0-7566-0835-4 paperback
ISBN 978-0-7566-0832-3 hardcover

Look what the critics are saying about DK Biography!

"…highly readable, worthwhile overviews for young people…" —*Booklist*

"This new series from the inimitable DK Publishing brings together the usual brilliant photography with a historian's approach to biography subjects." —*Ingram Library Services*